RIVERS AND PONDS

PAUL STERRY

HAMLYN

HOW TO USE THIS BOOK

FRESHWATER SHRIMP ▲
Gammarus pulex
L 20mm. Common among
silt in slow-flowing streams.
Does not survive in still
water. Swims on its side.

This guide covers over 200 species of freshwater plants, invertebrates, amphibians,
fish, birds and mammals, most of which can
be observed in the UK. The identification
pages (44–125) give the common English
name, followed by the scientific name in
italics. Length (L), wingspan (W) and height
(H) are in metres, centimetres and millimetres,
and additional useful information, such as
♂ (male) and ♀ (female), is given. The life
cycles of some insects and amphibians have
been included to show how development
occurs, and nymphs and larvae have been
shown wherever possible. The sexes are
similar unless otherwise stated.

The author and publishers would like to thank
the following individuals for their assistance in
the preparation of this book: Andrew Branson of
British Wildlife Publishing, Principal Consultant,
Sarah Castell, Designer and Maggi McCormick,
Editorial Consultant

Published in 1992 by
Hamlyn Children's Books
part of Reed International Books,
Michelin House, 81 Fulham Road,
London SW3 6RB

ISBN 0 600 57379 6

Printed in Hong Kong

SAFETY CODE

- DO NOT GO TO RIVERS AND PONDS
  ALONE, AND NEVER GO TO PLACES
  WITH DEEP WATER AND STEEP BANKS
  WITHOUT AN ADULT.
- ALWAYS TELL AN ADULT WHERE YOU
  ARE GOING, AND WHEN YOU WILL BE
  BACK.
- BE CAREFUL AT THE EDGES OF RIVERS
  AND STREAMS – THE BANKS CAN BE
  SLIPPERY.
- TREAT ALL WILDLIFE WITH RESPECT.
- IF YOU TAKE A DOG WITH YOU, MAKE
  SURE IT IS ON A LEAD.
- DO NOT DRINK WATER FROM A RIVER
  OR POND.

CONTENTS

LIFE IN WATER

Ponds, lakes and rivers are living environments. Beneath the surface and all around them we can find a varied range of animals, birds and insects worthy of study. Some pond animals, such as fish, spend their entire lives in water. Others, including many insects, only live in water in their young stages. However, each is perfectly adapted to its environment. Without clean, healthy water none of the aquatic plants and animals could survive. The presence of oxygen is one of the most important aspects of a healthy pond. It is a gas that is present in air, and which dissolves into water. Plants also produce oxygen by a process called photosynthesis. All animals need this to breathe.

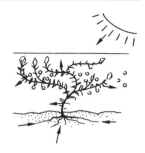

Plants are green because of a pigment called chlorophyll which traps sunlight energy and makes sugar and oxygen. This process is called photosynthesis.

This drawing shows a typical food chain in freshwater. At the top of the chain is the heron which catches fish. Fish eat freshwater shrimps which in turn eat tiny organisms. Each animal is dependent on each other in some way.

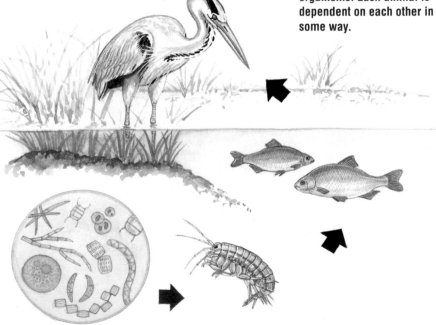

BREATHING METHODS

POND SNAIL   **WATER SCORPION**   **BEETLE**   **WATER LILY**

TUBIFEX WORM   **LEECH**   **BEETLE LARVA**   **NEWT**   **FISH**

TADPOLE

◁ Fish swim by moving their bodies from side to side. The tail fin provides the power behind this movement. The other fins keep it stable and help it change direction.

HOW TO WATCH

Many freshwater insects breathe air and regularly come to the surface of the water. Some, however, are truly aquatic. They use gills to take up oxygen dissolved in the water. Fully grown mayfly nymphs have seven pairs of gills on the side of the body. If you carefully place a nymph in some water against a black background, you will be able to see the gills beating regularly. Mayfly nymphs are very delicate. Always return them to their natural environment.

THE WORLD OF WATER

SURFACE
Water and air meet at the surface of a river or pond. Oxygen from the air dissolves in the water. This allows animals with gills to breathe.

MIDWATER
Many pond animals spend at least part of their lives in midwater. The most common creatures are fish, water beetles and water bugs.

PLANTS
Water plants are a sign of healthy freshwater. Many plants have their roots buried in the silt at the bottom of the pond, others float on the surface. Smaller pond animals will hide among water plants.

MUD AND SEDIMENT
Sediment often collects at the bottom of ponds, lakes and rivers. Mud or silt usually settles in ponds and lakes, while sand and gravel usually make up the beds of rivers and streams.

WHIRLYGIG BEETLE ▼
Gyrinus natator

GREAT DIVING BEETLE ▼
Dytiscus marginalis

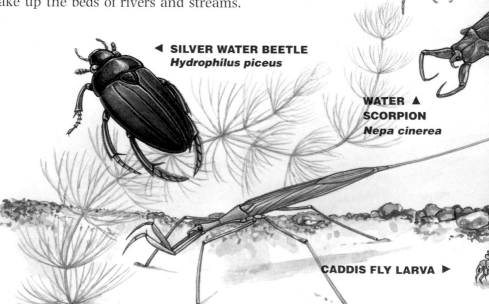

◄ SILVER WATER BEETLE
Hydrophilus piceus

WATER ▲ SCORPION
Nepa cinerea

CADDIS FLY LARVA ►

HORNWORT ▲
Ceratophyllum demersum

WATER STICK INSECT ▲
Ranatra linearis

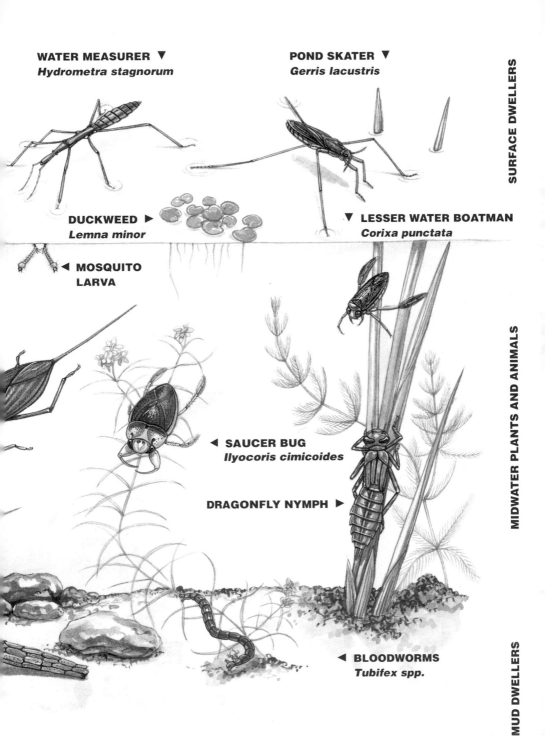

WATER MEASURER ▼
Hydrometra stagnorum

POND SKATER ▼
Gerris lacustris

DUCKWEED ▶
Lemna minor

▼ LESSER WATER BOATMAN
Corixa punctata

◀ MOSQUITO LARVA

◀ SAUCER BUG
Ilyocoris cimicoides

DRAGONFLY NYMPH ▶

◀ BLOODWORMS
Tubifex spp.

CLASSIFICATION

FLATWORM
Flat body without segments. Moves by a gliding motion. Some species may have eyespots.

LEECH
Body muscular and segmented. Sucker at head and tail end. Moves by looping the loop.

FRESHWATER CRUSTACEAN
Body protected by hard skin. Paired legs and feelers. Prominent eyes or eyespots.

FISH
Swim actively using fins. Body covered in hard scales. Spawns large numbers of eggs in spring and summer.

CLASSIFICATION

Animals and plants that belong to the same species share distinctive characteristics. Some of these characteristics can be used to see if different species are related to one another. For example, mayflies and moths are both classified as insects because, as adults, they share certain features. They both have bodies divided into three sections: the head, the thorax and the abdomen. They also have two pairs of wings and three pairs of legs. In some groups of animals that are classified together, their appearances may be very different. For example, swan mussels and ramshorn snails look very different. However, they both have soft bodies, protected by a hard shell, and are classified as molluscs.

FROG
Adults found on land and in water. Produce large masses of spawn. Tadpoles are aquatic.

NEWT
Adults can live on land or in water. Lizard-like appearance with a broad, flattened tail.

FRESHWATER MUSSEL
Shell in two halves protecting the soft body. Feeds and breathes by sucking in water.

WATER SNAIL
Soft body protected by a hard, spiral shell. Two tentacles, two eyes and a muscular foot.

DAMSELFLY
Adult has two pairs of similar veined wings. Nymph slender with three 'tails'.

DRAGONFLY
Adult has two pairs of wings and large eyes. Nymphs are predatory and have good eyesight.

STONEFLY
Adult has two pairs of wings folded over body at rest. Nymphs flat with two 'tails'.

IDENTIFICATION

It is important to be able to identify the plants and animals in the ponds and rivers that you visit. It enables you to compare the numbers of individuals from different species. You can then work out which are common and which are rare. Identification is not always easy. It often requires skill and a lot of experience. However, being able to identify species correctly is extremely satisfying. With each group of plants and animals there are usually a few important characteristics to look out for. For example, in insects the shape and colour of the wings is often critical. Sometimes the veins on the wings are also useful. Caddis fly larvae can be identified by the many different types of cases they construct.

CADDIS FLY
Adults are moth-like. Not very strong fliers. Larvae live in cases made from stones or plant material.

MAYFLY
Adults have two pairs of unequal wings. Short life. Nymphs have three 'tails'.

FLY (MOSQUITO)
Adults fly with one pair of wings. The second pair are reduced. Larvae and pupae are aquatic.

WATER BEETLE
Hard, shiny body. First pair of wings form hard cases to protect wings.

WATER BUG
Mouth-parts which pierce and suck, three pairs of legs and well developed eyes. Breathes air.

EQUIPMENT

CAREFUL HANDLING

All sorts of different freshwater creatures can be
seen by watching from the banks of a river or
pond. However, by using a variety of simple
items of equipment, you can see a whole lot
more when pond dipping. The most basic item
of equipment is the net. If the mesh is too fine
then the net will soon get clogged up with plant
debris and silt. If the mesh is too coarse then
many of the animals will escape. A mesh size of
1–2mm is usually the most suitable. You will
also need an array of trays, buckets and dishes
in which to put your catch. Pipettes, spoons and
paintbrushes are useful for moving the most
delicate creatures. A magnifying glass helps you
look at tiny animals and plants. Always take a
notebook in which to record what you find.

Equipment checklist
Long-handled net
Hand net
Sieve
Bucket
Sampling tray
Plastic tubs
Plastic spoons
Pipette
Paintbrush
Magnifying lens
Plastic screw-top jars
Plastic bags and ties
Notebook and pencil

Some pond animals have dark bodies and are easiest to see against a light background. Others have pale bodies and are best seen against a dark background. When you take a pond sample with a net you will have a mixture of both types. In order to be able to see both clearly you can make your own sampling tray. Buy a shallow, white plastic tray and paint one half black. Use paint that will not rub off in water. When you take a sample of pond life, move it around in the tray from time to time.

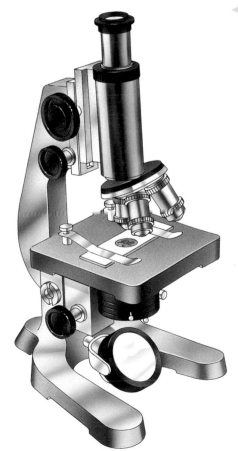

Microscopes are used to look at tiny plants and animals. Things that are invisible to the naked eye can be seen in this way. A series of glass lenses magnify the creatures under the microscope. A bright light is needed for totally clear viewing.

Ostracods, tiny crustaceans, are just big enough to be seen with the naked eye. Under the microscope, however, much more detail can be seen. The two shell-like cases which protect the body are clearly shown. These are covered in tiny hairs.

SAMPLING TECHNIQUES

Once you have collected all the pond dipping equipment you need you can set out on your first field trip. However, you will soon discover that there are good ways and bad ways of pond dipping. You must learn your sampling techniques. The most important item is the net. Do not use it if there is a dense growth of weed in the pond – it will be difficult to move the net through the water and fast swimming animals will be able to escape. Always have a sampling tray ready in which to put the contents of the net. If you collect too much material, it will be difficult to sort through it. Always remember to return all of your sample to the pond when you have finished. Most freshwater plants and animals will not survive long out of water.

DO...
- return your sample to the pond when you have finished.
- practice using your net.
- wash your hands thoroughly after handling samples.

DON'T...
- collect too much material.
- sample from areas of dense weed with a net.
- damage delicate animals by handling the sample roughly.
- go to rivers and ponds alone.

MAKING A NET

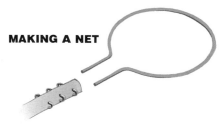

1. Bend some strong wire ▲ into a loop. Find a stout pole which will be the net handle.

3. Fold the net. Sew the ▼ sides of the net together to make a bag.

2. Cut a piece of net ▲ (mesh size 1–2mm) into a triangular shape as shown. Cut off the bottom.

4. Sew the top of the net ▼ around the wire loop. Attach the wire to one end of the pole (handle).

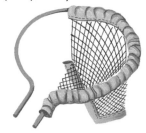

5. Make sure there are no ▲ large holes along the sewn edge and that the net is firmly tied to the pole.

Nets work best when the pond or river you are sampling does not have too much weed. Many creatures hide among floating plants and debris at the surface. These are best caught as follows. Gently submerge the net in the water until it is below the weed. Then quickly sweep upwards so that fast swimming creatures have no chance to escape. Animals that live among weed lower in the water are best caught using a sideways movement of the net.

To catch animals at the surface, a swift ◢ upwards movement of the net is the best method. By doing this, you give the creature no chance to escape.

A sideways movement through ◢ submerged weed is the best way of catch animals that normally live below the surface, such as a crayfish.

HOW TO WATCH

Many freshwater animals are surprisingly alert. They will often see you long before you see them and move away. When approaching a pond or river, make sure you keep a low profile so that your outline does not break the skyline. Sit quietly and patiently and wait. Fish will soon move into the open water and a dragonfly may settle in front of you.

SEASONS

Spring

Spring is the season of new growth in the pond. Fresh leaves appear on the water plants, and seeds begin to germinate. In early spring, frogs, toads and newts return to ponds and lakes. They mate and spawn in the shallows. Their tadpoles take several weeks before they become miniature adults. Later in the season, fish begin to spawn and insects such as dragonflies and mayflies emerge as adults from their nymphal stages. Animals that hibernated in the pond become active again. Water birds begin to nest.

Summer ▷

During the summer months, the plants grow to their full height. Many produce colourful flowers which attract insects to collect nectar. The eggs of waterbirds have hatched, and families of moorhens and coots can be seen. Young fish have hatched from their eggs and swim freely. Many are eaten by the inhabitants of the water. Dragonflies and other insects mate and lay their eggs in the water. Soon afterwards, the adults die. Water beetles and water bugs become numerous in the ponds and lakes.

Autumn

Autumn is the season when the plants begin to die. First the leaves on the trees turn brown. Then they fall and many collect on the bottom of ponds and lakes. Flowers that appeared in the summer now produce seeds and fruits. Frogs, toads and newts begin to leave the water and go in search of suitable hibernating places. Many adult insects die off. Their eggs or larvae survive the winter to become adults the following year. Some freshwater birds begin to leave in autumn.

Winter

For the pond watcher, winter is the quietest season. Most of the plants have died back. Freshwater animals are mostly hibernating or in resting stages in their life-cycles. In very cold weather, the surface of the pond may freeze over. As long as there is free water underneath, fish will still survive. Frogs, toads and newts are amphibians. They are equally at home on land or in water. In the winter, most leave the water and hibernate under stones or fallen logs.

RECORDS AND PHOTOGRAPHY

TAKING NOTES

It is a good idea to take notes when you go pond dipping, or are studying creatures in a tank at home. These may help you identify a plant or animal at a later date. The notes also make interesting reading in the months that follow. For example, you can record the time it takes for tadpoles to reach the different stages on the way from spawn to frog.

PHOTOGRAPHY

In the past, people who studied freshwater life had no way of recording their catch other than by taking notes, drawing or killing specimens. Nowadays, we are more lucky and we can take photographs. You can buy close-up (macro) lenses to fit most modern cameras. With these you can photograph insects at very close range.

The best type of camera to buy for wildlife photography is a 35mm SLR. There are many different makes available. You can fit many different types of lenses to them. Other, cheaper, cameras can also be used. It is also a good idea to use a tripod to support the camera when photographing in the field. It is particularly useful if you are waiting for something to happen and want to stay in one position. For example, it is useful when watching a dragonfly emerge.

Modern cameras, lenses and films are so good that anyone can take stunning photographs. These make wonderful records of your day out. Make sure you take lenses and equipment plus plenty of spare film.

HOW TO WATCH

Many birds are rather wary and can be difficult to photograph. However, photographers sometimes use the riverside vegetation to get close to their subject. Try and keep below the height of the vegetation so that you do not break the skyline. You should also move slowly so as not to frighten the bird. Another way to take photographs is to sit quietly with your camera set up.

MAKING A POND

A GARDEN POND

If you do not have a river or pond near you, making a garden pond can be a most rewarding exercise. It will give hours of pleasure to the household and will become a haven for wildlife. There are a few important things to consider before you design your pond. Try to site it away from trees and overhanging branches. In the autumn, the leaves will fall into the water and rot down. In the summer, the pond may be too shaded. Make the sides of the pond into gentle shelves so that frogs and other creatures can easily leave it if they want. Ensure that at least one part of the pond is more than 60cm deep. Even if the surface of the pond freezes over in winter, this deeper section should stay ice-free so that fish, and other permanent pond residents, will still be able to survive.

Garden nature reserves
Nowadays, many village ponds and other small pools have disappeared. This is partly due to neglect and partly to land drainage. Garden ponds are, therefore, important refuges for wildlife. They serve as unofficial nature reserves. The more new ponds are created, the better it will be for freshwater life. In particular, frogs and newts have greatly benefited from the creation of garden ponds. Many different water plants also thrive.

1. Dig a hole to the shape and depth you require. One part should be at least 60cm deep. The sides should shelve.

2. Line the hole with plastic sheeting. This can be bought in garden centres. Allow a margin of about 30cm around the edge.

3. Remove any sharp stones from beneath the plastic and then fill with water. Allow a day or so before stocking the pond with plants.

4. Cover the edge of the plastic with soil and plant the margin with marsh plants. Cover the bottom of the pond with silt and soil.

Stocking the pond
Plants and animals will colonize your new pond in time. However, you may want to speed things up. Many garden centres stock pond plants. Only buy from a reputable centre since some suppliers illegally remove plants from the wild. Ask a friend with a pond to give you surplus plants for your new pond. They may also give you frogspawn in the spring as well as pond insects and crustaceans. Only collect a small amount of frogspawn from the wild, and use pet shops for fish, etc.

AQUARIUMS

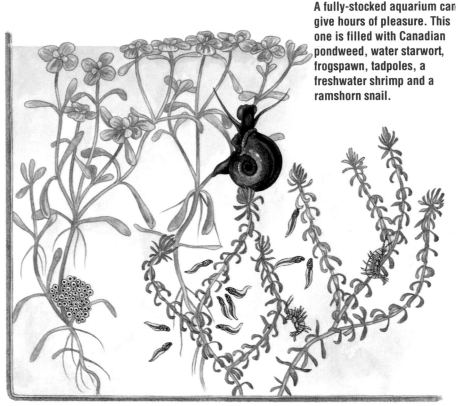

A fully-stocked aquarium can give hours of pleasure. This one is filled with Canadian pondweed, water starwort, frogspawn, tadpoles, a freshwater shrimp and a ramshorn snail.

STOCKING THE AQUARIUM

It is a good idea to have water plants in your tank. These produce oxygen, which many of the pond animals need to take up from the water. Plants such as Canadian pondweed and water starwort will usually thrive in an aquarium. Other species may prefer flowing water, and will not survive unless you use an aerator. Keep an eye on the condition of the water plants. If they look unhealthy, remove and replace them. Stock the aquarium with a wide range of pond animals. Introduce some silt, which will contain smaller animals and eggs of larger ones. Avoid having predators such as larger water beetles, since they may eat the other animals.

DO...
- keep the tank stocked with weed.
- remove silt and dead plants regularly.
- keep in a cool place.
- keep in a light room.
- provide sticks etc. for emerging insects to climb.
- keep the tank open to air but use a special lid if creatures are likely to jump out.

DON'T...
- keep in direct sunlight.
- overstock with animals.
- stock with predators.
- use a goldfish bowl.

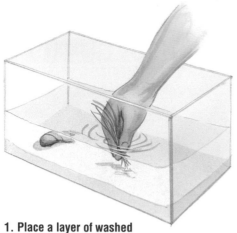

1. Place a layer of washed gravel or sand on the bottom of the tank, and arrange larger stones to give a natural appearance. Half fill with water before proceeding.

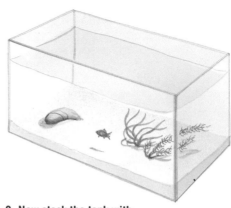

2. Now stock the tank with pondweeds. Tie the roots to a stone and bed them both into the gravel. The stone stops the weed from floating to the surface.

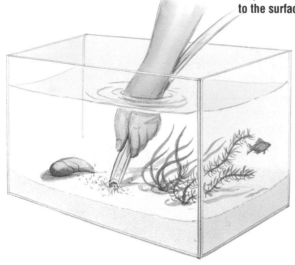

3. Add water to the tank slowly to prevent disturbance. Clean the tank from time to time using a siphon. Move the end of the tube over the gravel to suck up silt and debris.

HOW TO WATCH

Glass tanks allow you to watch freshwater animals behaving naturally, without having to join them in the water! This water boatman was photographed at the water's surface in a tank. The silvery appearance is due to air which covers its body.

CONSERVATION AND POLLUTION

POLLUTION

In years gone by, the major threat to areas of standing water, such as ponds and lakes, was neglect. They gradually filled in and were colonized by shrubs and trees. Today, pollution from the modern world is the most serious threat to all water bodies. Farming practices pollute the water with fertilizers and pesticides. Sewage and waste from industry is also discharged into rivers. On top of this, rivers and canals are often used as unofficial dumping sites for household waste. To improve matters, there are new laws to protect the environment. These are, however, difficult to enforce. We can all help as well. Organized groups always need help to clear rubbish from ponds and lakes. This should never be attempted on your own.

DO...
– return your pond samples to the water.
– watch for signs of pollution.

DON'T...
– pick wild flowers.
– cause too much disturbance either in the pond or on the bank.
– leave rubbish behind when you leave.
– take samples away that you cannot look after properly and cannot eventually return.

Frogs produce large quantities of spawn in the spring. The spawn contains lots of eggs. In nature, most of these die while they are still tadpoles. If you have spawn in your garden pond, keep a small amount in a jar with pond weeds and watch the tadpoles grow. Make sure the water is changed regularly. When they have become young froglets, you can then release them into your garden pond or a gravel pit and watch them as they grow into adult frogs.

Clearing canals

From time to time, canals have to be cleared. They become clogged with rubbish dumped by humans and can get overgrown and full of silt. The best way to do this for the wildlife of the canal is to clear short stretches at a time. This allows animals to quickly re-colonize. Unfortunately, canal clearance is sometimes done in an unsympathetic way by draining long stretches at one time. This often destroys the wildlife value of the canal. Always join an organized official group to clear canals – do not attempt this on your own!

One of the saddest sights to greet any freshwater naturalist is that of dead fish floating on the water. Fish take up oxygen dissolved in the water to breathe. One of the most frequent ways they are killed is when chemicals pollute the water and so encourage bacteria to use up the oxygen. Of course if fish die, then so also do many other water animals. Hopefully, tough laws controlling pollution may make this unhappy sight a thing of the past.

GARDEN PONDS

Garden ponds are wonderful habitats for the freshwater naturalist. They are literally right on the doorstep, and can be studied at leisure. They are easy to construct and it is fun to watch plants and animals colonize them. You can also try introducing creatures for yourself. Because lots of village ponds and other freshwater habitats have disappeared, garden ponds are important refuges for many plants and animals. In particular, frogs often do extremely well and produce lots of spawn. Garden ponds are usually small and do not have running water. Plants and animals that normally live in streams and rivers with flowing water do not survive well in garden ponds.

Arrowhead ▼
With its arrow-shaped leaves, this plant grows well in the garden pond. The leaves that grow underwater are long and grass-like.

Frogspawn ▼
In the spring, frogs come to the pond to mate and produce spawn. The jelly-like coating protects the developing tadpoles from any damage.

Canadian pondweed ▼
Introduced from North America, this plant flourishes in our ponds. It grows so quickly that it often has to be cleared in autumn.

Goldfish ▲
People often stock their garden pond with these attractive fish. If there are too many, however, the pond's other animals will suffer.

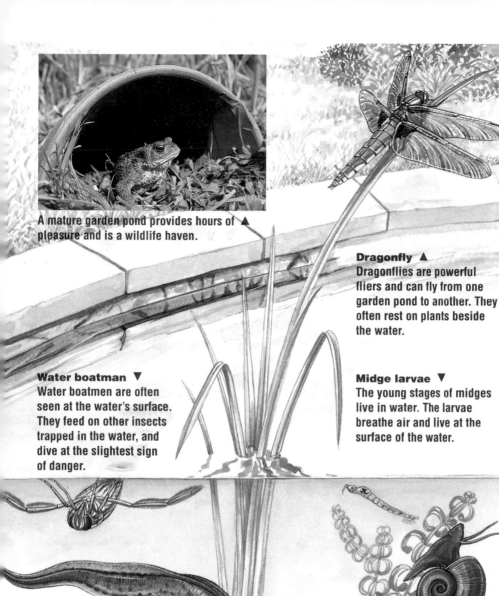

A mature garden pond provides hours of ▲
pleasure and is a wildlife haven.

Dragonfly ▲
Dragonflies are powerful
fliers and can fly from one
garden pond to another. They
often rest on plants beside
the water.

Water boatman ▼
Water boatmen are often
seen at the water's surface.
They feed on other insects
trapped in the water, and
dive at the slightest sign
of danger.

Midge larvae ▼
The young stages of midges
live in water. The larvae
breathe air and live at the
surface of the water.

Palmate newt ▶
Newts are easiest to see in
the spring when males and
females are courting. In the
autumn they leave the pond.

Ramshorn snail ▲
The spiral shell of the
ramshorn snail is easy to
recognize. They do well
in garden ponds.

VILLAGE PONDS

At one time, there would have been a pond in the middle of most villages, usually found near a crossroads or a farm. This was used for giving animals water. Nowadays, many of these ponds have been filled in or have become overgrown. Some have survived, however, and are now havens for wildlife. In order to keep the village pond healthy, they have to be cleared out from time to time. This stops silt and mud from choking the water plants. Pond clearing should only be done in the autumn and winter and only in an officially organized group. Sometimes the birds on village ponds become used to people feeding them and are rather tame. If the village pond is clean, many other water creatures will live there.

Duckweed ▼
This tiny plant has oval leaves that float on the surface of the pond. In summer, duckweed may cover the entire surface.

Pond skater ▶
These insects live on the surface of the water and skate around. They feed on flies and other creatures that fall into the water.

Common toad ▼
Toads come to the village pond in the spring to mate and produce spawn. They make a faint croaking call.

Great pond snail ▼
These large snails come to the surface of the water to breathe air. They feed on water plants.

Yellow flag iris ▼
This colourful plant grows around the margins of the pond. The bright yellow flowers attract insects.

The commonest duck on village ponds is ▲ the mallard. Males have colourful plumage. Females are plain brown.

Moorhen ▲
Moorhens are rather shy birds. They prefer ponds with patches of waterside vegetation where they can hide if disturbed.

Great diving beetle ▲
The great diving beetle is a powerful swimmer. It can sometimes be seen at the surface of the water.

◄ **Water scorpion**
This water bug is difficult to see when it is in the water. It looks like a leaf and moves very slowly.

UPLAND LAKES

Upland lakes often look bleak and windswept, the surface often freezing in the winter. Despite the harsh environment, however, they still harbour a variety of plants and animals. Compared to lowland lakes, the waters are generally cold and poor in nutrients and the lakes are often deep. Plants do not grow as well as in lakes of a similar size in lowland areas. Upland lakes are often a long way from other lakes and separated by mountains or hills. Because they can fly, birds and insects can usually reach them. Upland lakes usually only have a few species of fish since most cannot tolerate the cold waters.

Stonefly ▲
Stoneflies can be common in upland lakes. The nymphs live in the water. The adults crawl over stones around the edge of the lake.

Tufted duck ▶
These are diving ducks. They are most common on upland lakes in winter, but they leave if the water freezes.

Leech ▶
Several species of leeches are found in upland lakes.

Perch ▲
These elegant fish live in all sorts of lakes except the most inhospitable. They are active predators and feed on insects and smaller fish.

Caddis fly larva ▶
Several species live in upland lakes. The larvae make their cases from particles of sand and small shell fragments.

Common blue damselfly
The nymphs live in the water and feed on small animals. The adults are often seen resting on rushes.

Coot ▶
They may breed on the lake in small numbers. Large flocks may form in the winter months. They dive well and feed on underwater vegetation.

◀ **Bogbean**
This plant is common around many lakes. It sometimes forms large patches. The leaves resemble those of a broad bean.

◀ **Rushes**
Rushes have slender, spiky leaves and grow in clumps. They are found in shallow water and on boggy ground. There are several species.

LOWLAND LAKES

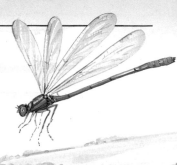

Lowland lakes are rich in wildlife. The water is often shallow and gets warm in the summer months. Water plants flourish and there is usually plenty of vegetation around the edge of the lake; there may be shrubs and trees, or sometimes a reed-bed. A thick layer of silt often collects on the bottom. Lowland lakes are particularly good for water insects such as dragonflies, damselflies, water bugs and water beetles. Many different kinds of fish also thrive there, and spawning shoals can be seen in the early summer. Birds are attracted to lowland lakes. Some, such as herons and kingfishers, feed on fish while others, such as swans and geese, feed on plants.

Large red damselfly ▲
This attractive insect is often seen resting on reeds and other plants. Look out for mating pairs.

Water lily ▲
By the end of the summer, some lowland lakes are covered with lily leaves. The white flowers appear in June and July. Fish may hide under the leaves.

Canada goose ▲
Family parties are often seen in the summer months. In flight, they make a loud honking call.

Common reed ▲
Reeds grow in shallow water around the edge of the lake. Sometimes, large patches may form and these are called reed-beds.

◀ **Water spider**
The water spider looks silvery under water. This is due to air trapped around its body, which is used for breathing.

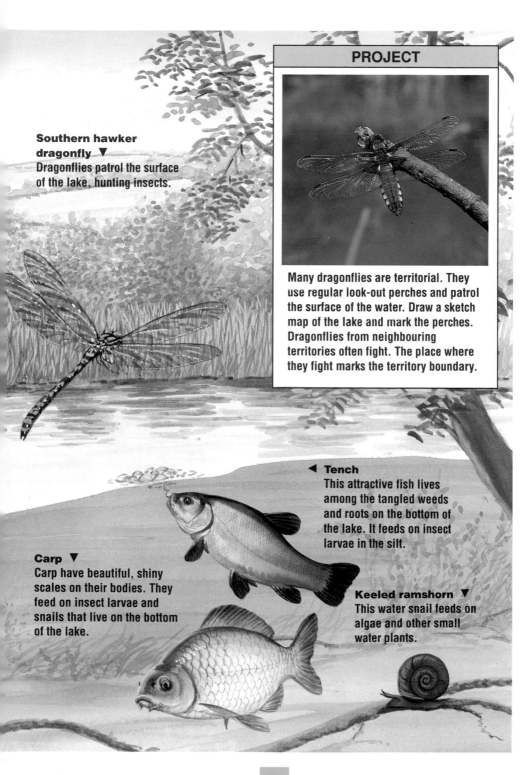

Southern hawker dragonfly ▼
Dragonflies patrol the surface of the lake, hunting insects.

Many dragonflies are territorial. They use regular look-out perches and patrol the surface of the water. Draw a sketch map of the lake and mark the perches. Dragonflies from neighbouring territories often fight. The place where they fight marks the territory boundary.

◀ **Tench**
This attractive fish lives among the tangled weeds and roots on the bottom of the lake. It feeds on insect larvae in the silt.

Carp ▼
Carp have beautiful, shiny scales on their bodies. They feed on insect larvae and snails that live on the bottom of the lake.

Keeled ramshorn ▼
This water snail feeds on algae and other small water plants.

GRAVEL PITS

Gravel pits are man-made habitats. Gravel is extracted from the ground and used to build roads and buildings. When the pits are abandoned, they soon fill with water. Sometimes anglers stock them with fish, but most of the creatures that live in the gravel pit get there naturally. Birds are often the first to arrive, and ducks, coots and grebes are frequently seen. Water plants colonize the edge of the water, and dragonflies and other insects follow afterwards. Many other freshwater habitats, such as ponds and lakes, have been destroyed or damaged in recent years, and gravel pits offer new environments for the plants and animals to live in. Some have been turned into nature reserves.

Great crested grebe ▶
These elegant birds build floating nests among the reeds. They dive for fish.

Pochard ▲
Pochards are diving ducks. Males have red heads and silvery-grey backs, females are brown. They gather in flocks in the winter.

Purple loosestrife ▶
A colourful plant that grows at the water's edge. It is often one of the first to colonize a new gravel pit.

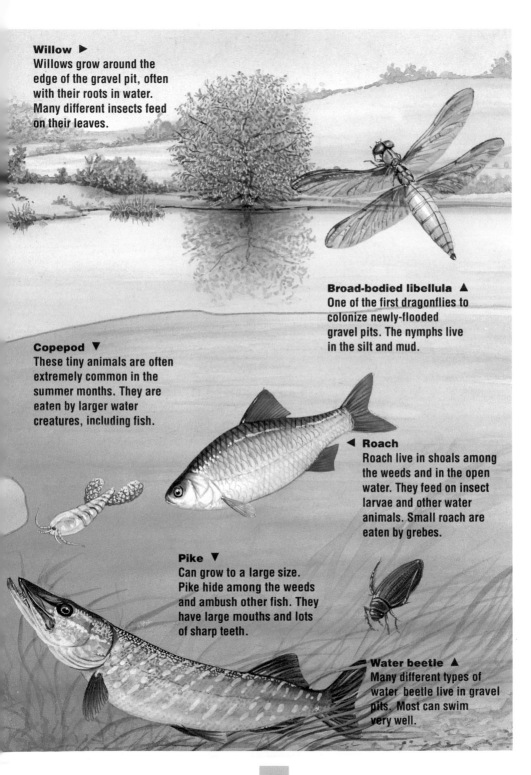

Willow ▶
Willows grow around the edge of the gravel pit, often with their roots in water. Many different insects feed on their leaves.

Broad-bodied libellula ▲
One of the first dragonflies to colonize newly-flooded gravel pits. The nymphs live in the silt and mud.

Copepod ▼
These tiny animals are often extremely common in the summer months. They are eaten by larger water creatures, including fish.

◀ **Roach**
Roach live in shoals among the weeds and in the open water. They feed on insect larvae and other water animals. Small roach are eaten by grebes.

Pike ▼
Can grow to a large size. Pike hide among the weeds and ambush other fish. They have large mouths and lots of sharp teeth.

Water beetle ▲
Many different types of water beetle live in gravel pits. Most can swim very well.

UPLAND RIVERS

Upland rivers are fast flowing. The water often crashes over boulders, and deep pools can sometimes form. The river bed is usually made up of gravel and sand, so only plants that have strong roots can survive, otherwise they would get washed away by the speed of the current. Because upland rivers are usually in remote areas, they do not suffer from as much pollution as other rivers. Many of the small animals that live in the river have hard cases to protect them from damage. Some of them are attached to boulders and rocks to stop them being swept away. At certain times of year – often in spring and autumn – the river flow increases dramatically due to heavy rains.

River limpet ▼
Groups of conical shells can be found on the downstream side of boulders. They will move if the current changes.

Water louse ▼
The water louse lives on the bed of the river. The gravel and sand provide protection from the current.

Caddis fly larva ▶
Several different species of caddis fly larva live in upland rivers. They make cases from sand and twigs.

Brown trout ▲
Brown trout often live in deep pools that form behind boulders or beneath small waterfalls.

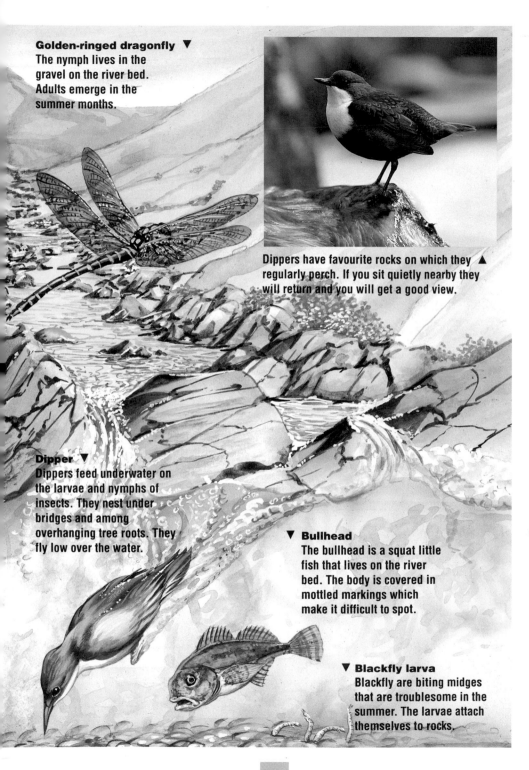

Golden-ringed dragonfly ▼
The nymph lives in the gravel on the river bed. Adults emerge in the summer months.

Dippers have favourite rocks on which they ▲ regularly perch. If you sit quietly nearby they will return and you will get a good view.

Dipper ▼
Dippers feed underwater on the larvae and nymphs of insects. They nest under bridges and among overhanging tree roots. They fly low over the water.

▼ **Bullhead**
The bullhead is a squat little fish that lives on the river bed. The body is covered in mottled markings which make it difficult to spot.

▼ **Blackfly larva**
Blackfly are biting midges that are troublesome in the summer. The larvae attach themselves to rocks.

LOWLAND RIVERS

Lowland rivers are often broad and deep. The water flows at a slower speed than in an upland river, so more plants and animals can survive. However, the water is usually not as clear in the lowland river. The river's course often winds through the countryside, where insect life is abundant. In the spring, thousands of mayflies emerge and fly for a few days in large swarms. Dragonflies and damselflies are also common among waterside vegetation. Their nymphs live in the water and hide among water plants. Lowland rivers also support lots of different fish, which feed on plants and animals. Birds such as kingfishers and herons feed on the fish.

Banded demoiselle ▲ damselfly
The wings of this attractive insect have a metallic sheen which catches the light.

Mayfly ▲
Adult mayflies only live for a day or two. They usually fly at dusk in large swarms. When they die they fall onto water and are eaten by fish.

Freshwater shrimp ▶
Freshwater shrimps live around the roots of water plants on the river bed. They are a favourite food for many of the river's fish.

Freshwater crayfish ▼
Crayfish resemble miniature lobsters. They live under stones and among roots. If alarmed, they swim backwards.

Flatworm ▲
Flatworms move by gliding smoothly over the river bed. They feed on small animals. Do not have proper eyes, but are sensitive to light.

Kingfishers are the most colourful birds ▲
to be seen on the lowland river. Their
plumage is a mixture of blue and orange.
They nest in burrows in the bank.

◀ **Little grebe**
Little grebes dive for fish.
When alarmed they make a
trilling call. The nest is made
of floating vegetation.

Grayling ▼
This fish does not like
polluted waters. It prefers
parts of the river with a good
water flow. Grayling feed on
insect larvae and nymphs.

Otter ▼
Otters are now quite rare.
Sadly, they were persecuted
by man in the past; now they
are protected by the law.

◀ **Water vole**
Sometimes incorrectly
called 'water rats', these
charming animals make
burrows in the river bank.
They feed on the shoots of
water plants.

LOWLAND STREAMS

Some streams arise from springs in low-lying parts of the country, often in areas where the soil is chalk. Lowland streams are usually shallow and wide. They occasionally flood, so the land beside them is often boggy and full of marsh plants. During the summer months, there is often a rich growth of water plants. These die back into the water in winter. The larvae and nymphs of insects live among the weeds. If the stream runs over chalk, there may be several species of water snail present. They use the calcium in the chalk to make their shells. Fish such as minnows and sticklebacks live in the shallow water. Brown trout also like these streams and spawn in the shallows.

Water crowfoot ▼
Long strands of crowfoot grow in the swift current. In the summer, white flowers with five petals are produced.

▼ Water measurer
The water measurer glides across the surface of the water. It feeds on other insects trapped there.

Water milfoil ▶
The feathery leaves are arranged in whorls around the stem. Large patches grow in slow-flowing stretches.

Minnow ▲
Shoals of minnows live in slow-flowing parts of the stream. They spawn in the shallows and feed on small water insects.

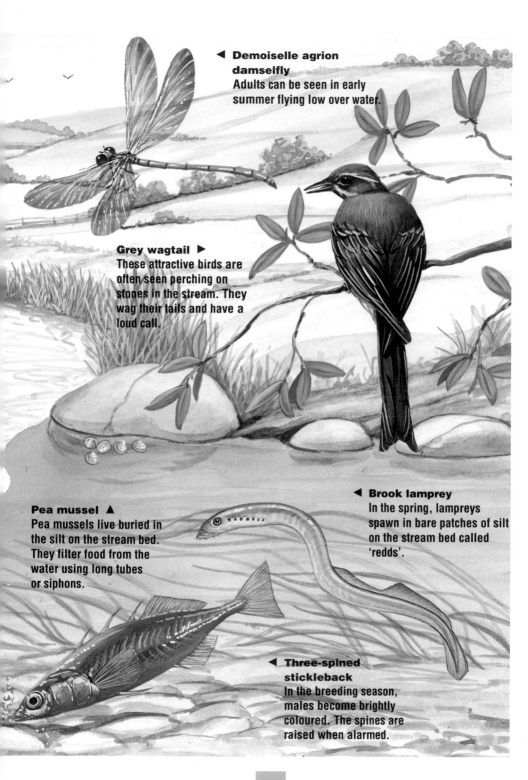

◄ Demoiselle agrion damselfly
Adults can be seen in early summer flying low over water.

Grey wagtail ►
These attractive birds are often seen perching on stones in the stream. They wag their tails and have a loud call.

◄ Brook lamprey
In the spring, lampreys spawn in bare patches of silt on the stream bed called 'redds'.

Pea mussel ▲
Pea mussels live buried in the silt on the stream bed. They filter food from the water using long tubes or siphons.

◄ Three-spined stickleback
In the breeding season, males become brightly coloured. The spines are raised when alarmed.

CANALS

In the last century, many canals were built in order to transport goods across the country. The canal barges were pulled by horses, so there was comparatively little disturbance to the wildlife. Many of these canals are now derelict, but some have survived and a few are still good environments for wildlife. Unfortunately, on some canals that are used by boats today, there is a lot of disturbance. The water in canals flows only very slowly. This can be good for frogs, newts and fishes. If they have not been recently dredged, there is often a good growth of water plants. The nymphs and larvae of all sorts of insects live among the weeds.

Alderfly ▼
Alderflies are often seen resting on the leaves of waterside plants. Larvae live in the water and look rather like beetle larvae.

Grass snake ▼
They are quite at home in the water and swim well. Grass snakes feed on frogs and fish. Recognized by the yellow patches on their neck which look like a collar.

▼ Rudd
Rudd like the still or slow-flowing waters found in canals. They live in shoals and often feed near the surface of the water.

Bream ▶
Bream live in shoals and are usually found among water plants. They feed on insect larvae and other small water creatures.

◀ Silver diving beetle
This large species is rather a poor swimmer. It can sometimes be seen at the surface collecting air.

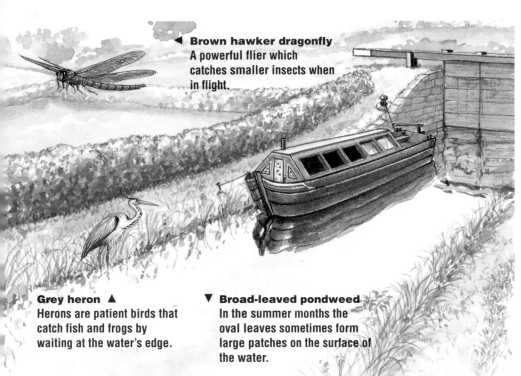

Brown hawker dragonfly
A powerful flier which catches smaller insects when in flight.

Grey heron ▲
Herons are patient birds that catch fish and frogs by waiting at the water's edge.

▼ **Broad-leaved pondweed**
In the summer months the oval leaves sometimes form large patches on the surface of the water.

Flowering rush ▶
This is now a rather scarce species. Flowering rush grows along the edge of the canal in marshy ground.

HOW TO WATCH

Sit quietly beside a canal in which lots of frogs and fish live. You may see a grass snake in the water. Watch its head closely when it comes to the surface. It frequently puts out its tongue to sample the air. Special organs in its mouth and the tongue are used to 'taste' the air.

MARSHY BOGS

Marshy bogs are found in areas of high rainfall, such as upland moors and heaths. The soil is often sandy and the water is acidic. There are pools of open water, but even the surrounding land is water-laden and boggy underfoot. Only plants that like to have their roots permanently wet can live here. Marshy bogs are often good for dragonflies and water bugs but few water snails can be found there. The water bugs live their entire lives in the water, but only the nymphal stages of the dragonflies are aquatic. In winter, much of the vegetation dies back, and a thick layer of dead plants can be found in the pools, with water creatures lurking at the bottom.

Sphagnum moss ▼
Sphagnum grows in dense cushions in the marsh bog. Sometimes it actually grows in the water.

Rushes ◀
These spiky leaved plants grow in clumps around the margins of pools. They are tough and few animals can eat them.

Bladderwort ▶
Bladderwort grows in marshy pools. Yellow flowers grow on spikes above the water. Small bladders on the stems catch tiny water creatures used for food.

Smooth newt ▲
In the spring, newts gather in the pools to mate. Females lay their eggs on the leaves of water plants.

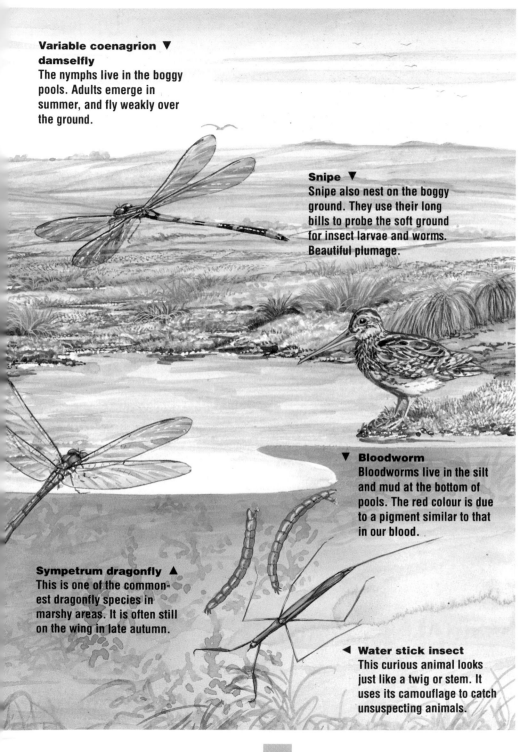

Variable coenagrion ▼ damselfly
The nymphs live in the boggy pools. Adults emerge in summer, and fly weakly over the ground.

Snipe ▼
Snipe also nest on the boggy ground. They use their long bills to probe the soft ground for insect larvae and worms. Beautiful plumage.

▼ Bloodworm
Bloodworms live in the silt and mud at the bottom of pools. The red colour is due to a pigment similar to that in our blood.

Sympetrum dragonfly ▲
This is one of the commonest dragonfly species in marshy areas. It is often still on the wing in late autumn.

◄ Water stick insect
This curious animal looks just like a twig or stem. It uses its camouflage to catch unsuspecting animals.

FLATWORMS AND TRUE WORMS

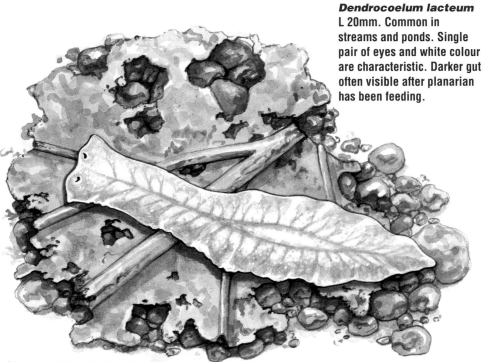

FLATWORM
Dendrocoelum lacteum
L 20mm. Common in streams and ponds. Single pair of eyes and white colour are characteristic. Darker gut often visible after planarian has been feeding.

CHARACTERISTICS

Flatworms are a primitive group of animals. Some of them are parasites and live inside other animals. The planarians, or triclads, are free-living in freshwater and easier to see. Planarians are not related to leeches which are in fact true worms. The easiest way to tell them apart is by the fact that planarians do not have suckers.

HABITS

The different species of planarians live in all sorts of freshwater habitats. They often hide under leaves and stones and when disturbed contract into a jelly-like blob. However, when they move they become flattened. The body is covered in tiny hairs called cilia. These beat and allow the animal to glide over stones and plants.

Planarians are carnivorous and eat water insects and crustaceans. The mouth can take in small animals whole. Larger ones are wrapped in slime and eaten bit by bit.

FLATWORM
Polycelis nigra
L 10mm. Common in still waters such as ponds and ditches. Large number of eyespots around head end. No tentacles.

FLATWORM ▷
Crenobia alpina
L 15mm. Lives in upland rivers and lakes and prefers cool water. Moves upstream in summer. Two tentacles at head end.

PROJECT

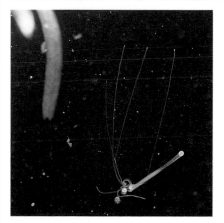

Hydra is not a flatworm but is similar to a small, slender sea anemone. They have long stinging tentacles which catch small water animals. These are moved to the mouth and swallowed. *Hydra* holds on to plants with the base of its body. It moves by looping-the-loop with its tentacles or somersaulting. To watch *Hydra*, put some pondweed in a tank. The animals soon move on to the glass. Stock the tank with small animals and watch the *Hydra* feed.

FLATWORM ▲
Dugesia lugubris
L 20mm. Two dark eye spots in white patches at head end. Regenerates easily if it is damaged.

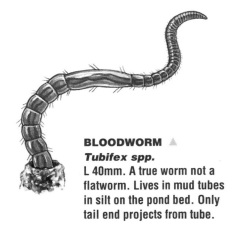

BLOODWORM ▲
Tubifex spp.
L 40mm. A true worm not a flatworm. Lives in mud tubes in silt on the pond bed. Only tail end projects from tube.

TRUE WORMS

CHARACTERISTICS

There are many different types of true worms found in freshwater. They all have bodies that are divided into segments. Although they have soft bodies, the outer skin is tough. Those on this page have bristles in each segment. The bristles allow them to grip the inside of their burrows and help them move. They have both male and female organs.

HABITS AND HABITATS

Most of the true worms, or Annelids, that live in freshwater are found in the mud and silt at the bottom of ponds, ditches and slow-flowing streams. They live in mud burrows, which helps protect their soft bodies. Most feed on small particles of food in the mud. Worms are important in recycling waste matter.

Look closely at a freshwater worm through a magnifying glass. You will see that each segment of the body has a cluster of bristles arranged in pairs, one on each side of the body. As it moves, it uses these bristles to grip on to whatever it is moving across.

SQUARE-TAILED WORM
Eiseniella tetrahedra
L 50mm. Lives in silt around lake edges and in slow-flowing rivers. Looks like a small earthworm.

WORM
Chaetogaster spp.
L 10mm. Body is pale and so internal organs are visible. Common among silt and mud on bottom of ponds.

WORM ▷
Nais spp.
L 25mm. Common and widespread. Lives in tubes in the silt of pond beds. Dorsal bristles long. Abdomen bristles short and in bunches.

WORM
Lumbriculus variegatus
L 70mm. Common in mud tubes which it makes in ponds, lakes and ditches. Body is greenish. Red pigment of blood seen.

WORM ▷
Stylaria spp.
L 15mm. Found among water plants. Head end has characteristic pointed proboscis. Hairs in segments are long and hair-like.

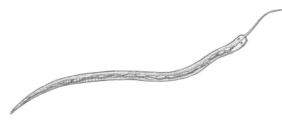

POTWORM
Enchytraeus spp.
L 25mm. Found among plant roots which they resemble. Sometimes live out of water where conditions are damp and moist.

LEECHES

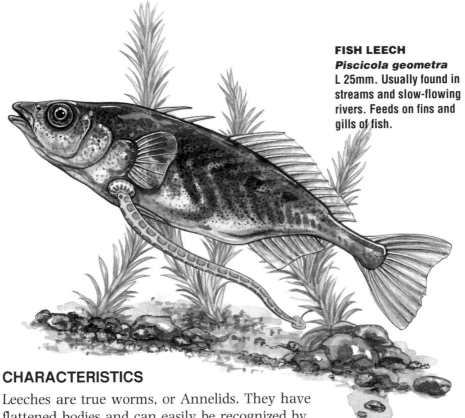

FISH LEECH
Piscicola geometra
L 25mm. Usually found in
streams and slow-flowing
rivers. Feeds on fins and
gills of fish.

CHARACTERISTICS

Leeches are true worms, or Annelids. They have
flattened bodies and can easily be recognized by
the suckers that are found at either end of the
body. Some species have stripes or spots on the
bodies and these are useful in identification.
Leeches have eye spots at the head. The
arrangement of these is different in each species.

HABITS

Leeches feed on the body fluids of other animals.
They attach themselves to their prey with their
suckers. Some species eat small pond animals
whole. Leeches are found in all sorts of
freshwater habitats. They often hide under
stones and among plants. Leeches occasionally
swim in an undulating way, but usually move
using their suckers.

The fish leech can often be
found on sticklebacks. It
attaches itself to the body
with its suckers. The mouth
is found in the head sucker. A
sharp proboscis is used to
pierce soft areas such as
gills and the base of fins.

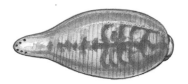

LEECH
Glossiphonia heteroclita
L 15mm. Most often found in still water. Three pairs of eyes. Feeds on water snails. Usually pale in colour.

LEECH
Glossiphonia complanata
L 15mm. Common and widespread in ponds, ditches and slow-flowing streams. Three pairs of eyes. Curls into a ball when disturbed.

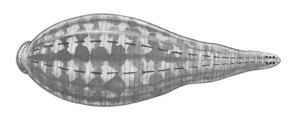

LEECH
Hemiclepsis marginata
L 15mm. A parasite of fish. Seldom found with *Piscicola* because it prefers ponds and other small water bodies. Two pairs of eyes.

LEECH
Helobdella stagnalis
L 10mm. Common and widespread in ponds and slow-flowing streams. Feeds on water snails and worms. One pair of eyes.

HORSE LEECH
Haemopsis sanguisuga
L 50mm. Fairly common in still water. An active predator. Eats whole worms, snails and crustaceans. Five pairs of eyes.

WATER FLEAS

CHARACTERISTICS

Water fleas and their relatives belong to a group of animals called crustaceans. Their soft bodies are protected by hard cases. They have jointed legs which are arranged in pairs. At the head end there are feelers and mouthparts which help sense the environment and enable them to feed. Water fleas and their relatives have simple eyes.

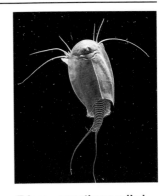

Triops – sometimes called *Apus* – only lives in pools that dry up in the summer. When these become wet in autumn and winter, the eggs hatch and grow quickly. *Triops* looks like a miniature horseshoe crab.

HABITS AND HABITATS

Water fleas and other small crustaceans are common in all sorts of water bodies. Many of them live in the open water and are important as food for small fish. Some, such as the ostracods, live on the bottom. Their bodies are protected by two shells rather like a small mussel. Most water fleas are more common in the summer months.

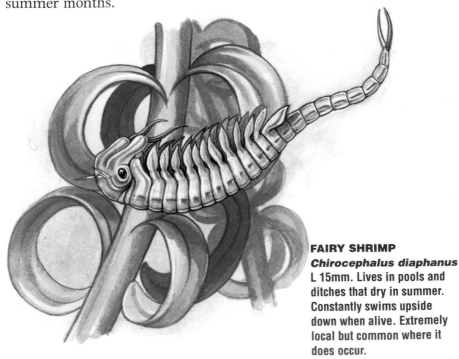

FAIRY SHRIMP
Chirocephalus diaphanus
L 15mm. Lives in pools and ditches that dry in summer. Constantly swims upside down when alive. Extremely local but common where it does occur.

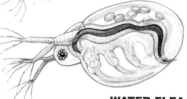

WATER FLEA
Daphnia magna
L 2.5mm. Lives in open water in ponds and lakes. Swims with jerky movement. Transparent body.

WATER FLEA ▽
Bosmina longirostris
L 1mm. Found in open water in ponds and lakes. Transparent body protected by shell plates.

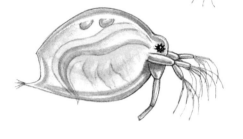

WATER FLEA ▲
Simocephalus spp.
L 3mm. Common and widespread in ponds and lakes. Lives among water plants. Swims jerkily.

OSTRACOD ▲
Cypridopsis vidua
L 1.5mm. Common in ponds, living on the bottom sediment. Pied markings are characteristic. Gathers in large numbers around food.

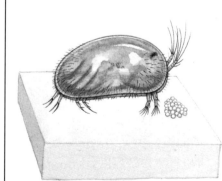

PROJECT

Ostracods can easily be reared in captivity. Put some jelly in a jar of pond water. Introduce a few ostracods and record the number. They eat the jelly and lay their eggs on it. Note their numbers every two weeks. Try the experiment with different types of water to see which they prefer.

OSTRACOD ▲
Herpetocypris spp.
L 2.5mm. Common among the sediments of ponds and lakes. Swims using its antennae. Eggs laid in clusters on plants.

WATER LOUSES

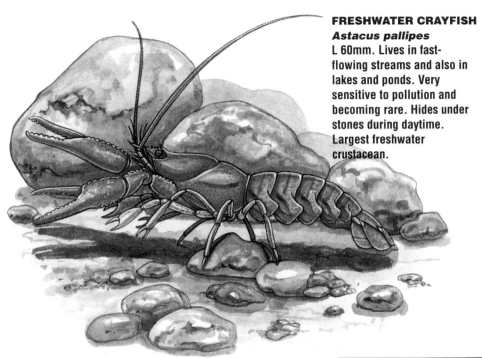

FRESHWATER CRAYFISH
Astacus pallipes
L 60mm. Lives in fast-flowing streams and also in lakes and ponds. Very sensitive to pollution and becoming rare. Hides under stones during daytime. Largest freshwater crustacean.

CHARACTERISTICS

The animals on this page are crustaceans. Their soft bodies are protected by a hard outer casing – the exoskeleton. Cyclops and copepods are small and best seen with a hand lens. The others are larger and easy to see. The freshwater shrimp and the water louse have poorly developed eyes. The freshwater crayfish, however, has large eyes.

HABITS

Crustaceans can be found in all sorts of different freshwater habitats. Cyclops and copepods live in open water and sometimes gather in large numbers near the surface. The freshwater crayfish, the water louse and the freshwater shrimp live on the bottom of streams and ponds.

During the summer months, female cyclops can be seen carrying two dark objects either side of their tail appendage. These are the egg sacs and contain hundreds of developing young stages. Eventually, these hatch out.

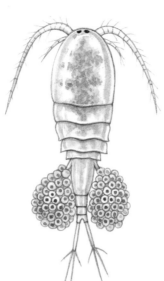

CYCLOPS
Cyclops spp.
L 2mm. Common in ponds and lakes. Found in open water. Swims with jerky movement. Females carry paired egg sacs.

WATER LOUSE ▽
Asellus aquaticus
L 20mm. Lives among plant roots and silt in slow-flowing streams and ponds. Moves by crawling. It is often eaten by fish.

FISH LOUSE ▷
Argulus foliaceus
L 6mm. Parasite of fish. Difficult to see when attached to fins or scales. Can swim freely to find new host. Often several are found on one fish.

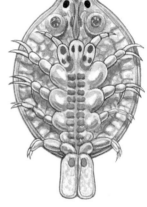

FRESHWATER SHRIMP ▷
Gammarus pulex
L 20mm. Common among silt in slow-flowing streams. Does not survive in still water. Swims on its side.

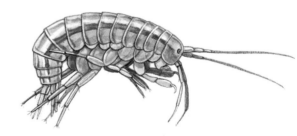

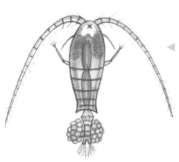

COPEPOD
Diaptomus castor
L 2mm. Common and widespread in ponds. Usually seen in early spring. Long antennae are characteristic. Swims with a jerky movement.

DAMSELFLIES

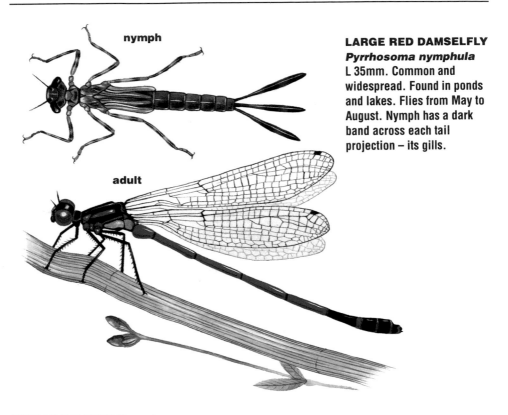

nymph

adult

LARGE RED DAMSELFLY
Pyrrhosoma nymphula
L 35mm. Common and widespread. Found in ponds and lakes. Flies from May to August. Nymph has a dark band across each tail projection – its gills.

INTRODUCTION

Damselflies belong to a group of animals called insects. The young stages – called nymphs – live in the water, while the adults are terrestrial and fly around over ponds and streams. Damselflies, like many other insects, are able to fly. Insects are the only group of invertebrates – animals without backbones – that can fly. Adult damselflies have two pairs of wings. The front wing is almost the same as the hind wing in shape. They are supported by a network of veins. The wings of most damselflies are transparent. They have good eyesight. Damselflies have two large eyes which are almost spherical in shape. These give almost all-round vision.

Some water insects come to the surface to breathe air. Others, such as damselfly nymphs, use gills to breathe oxygen in the water. Nymphs have three flattened projections at the tail end – these are the gills. These occasionally get broken off or damaged.

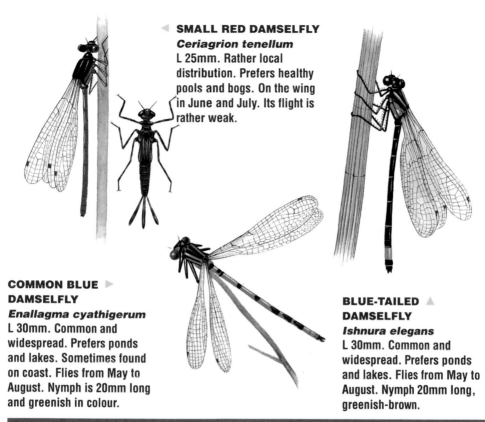

SMALL RED DAMSELFLY
Ceriagrion tenellum
L 25mm. Rather local distribution. Prefers healthy pools and bogs. On the wing in June and July. Its flight is rather weak.

COMMON BLUE ▷
DAMSELFLY
Enallagma cyathigerum
L 30mm. Common and widespread. Prefers ponds and lakes. Sometimes found on coast. Flies from May to August. Nymph is 20mm long and greenish in colour.

BLUE-TAILED △
DAMSELFLY
Ishnura elegans
L 30mm. Common and widespread. Prefers ponds and lakes. Flies from May to August. Nymph 20mm long, greenish-brown.

HOW TO WATCH

The young stages of damselflies are called nymphs and live in water. Adults can be seen flying during the summer months. After mating, female damselflies lay their eggs in the water. Some specics insert them into plants as protection. The eggs hatch into nymphs which feed on smaller pond animals. The nymphs are ready to hatch into adults in the spring. They climb up a stem out of the water and their skin splits. The adult damselfly emerges and pumps up its wings before they harden, often at night.

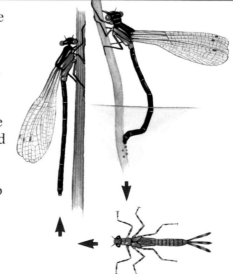

DAMSELFLIES

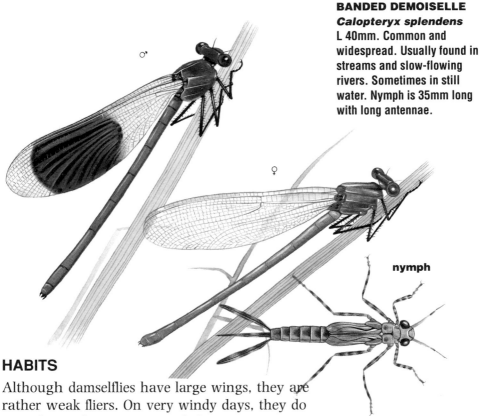

BANDED DEMOISELLE
Calopteryx splendens
L 40mm. Common and widespread. Usually found in streams and slow-flowing rivers. Sometimes in still water. Nymph is 35mm long with long antennae.

♂

♀

nymph

HABITS

Although damselflies have large wings, they are rather weak fliers. On very windy days, they do not take to the wing. Instead they rest among the vegetation. The nymphs usually move by creeping slowly through the water plants. If disturbed, they can swim actively by moving their bodies from side to side.

HABITATS AND FEEDING

Damselflies are found in all sorts of different freshwater habitats. Ponds and lakes have the most species and pools on boggy heaths are also good. A few species live in streams and rivers. The nymphs live buried in the silt at the bottom to stop them being washed away. Damselflies are predators. Adults catch flies, nymphs eat pond animals.

Most damselflies are smaller than dragonflies but otherwise they look rather similar. However, at rest, damselflies hold their wings vertically over their bodies. Dragonflies hold their wings out flat.

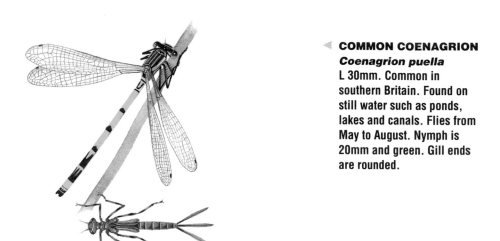

COMMON COENAGRION
Coenagrion puella
L 30mm. Common in southern Britain. Found on still water such as ponds, lakes and canals. Flies from May to August. Nymph is 20mm and green. Gill ends are rounded.

GREEN LESTES
Lestes sponsa
L 35mm. Widespread but local. Prefers ponds and canals. Body and wings have metallic green-bronze sheen. Flies in July and August. Nymph 30mm long.

VARIABLE COENAGRION
Coenagrion pulchellum
L 30mm. Common and widespread around ponds, lakes and canals. Fluttering flight. On the wing from May to August. Nymph is 20mm long and brownish.

BEAUTIFUL DEMOISELLE
Calopteryx virgo
L 40mm. Common, especially in the south. Prefers streams and slow-flowing rivers, but sometimes found in ponds and lakes. Metallic blue sheen to body and wings. Nymphs 35mm long.

DRAGONFLIES

INTRODUCTION

Like other insects, dragonflies have a body which is divided into three sections – the head, the thorax and the abdomen. Three pairs of legs are attached to the thorax, and the adults have two pairs of wings. At rest they hold their wings flat instead of folded over their body.

GENERAL FEATURES

Adult dragonflies have large eyes, which give them good vision. The species on these pages are all large and active fliers. Their wings are transparent and supported by a network of veins. Males and females often have different markings. The colour of an adult dragonfly's body changes colour as it gets older. Most adult species live for a few weeks.

Dragonfly nymphs are active carnivores. They feed on other insects, but can catch tadpoles or even small fish. On the underside of the head is a flap called the mask. This is armed with sharp jaws and fangs. At rest it is folded, but it can shoot out to catch prey.

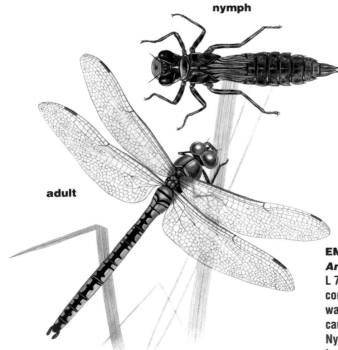

nymph

adult

EMPEROR DRAGONFLY
Anax imperator
L 70mm. Widespread and common on areas of still water such as lakes and canals. Powerful fliers. Nymphs 50mm long with large eyes and flattened head.

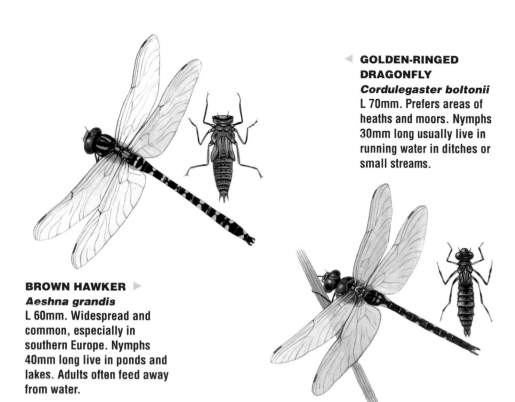

GOLDEN-RINGED DRAGONFLY
Cordulegaster boltonii
L 70mm. Prefers areas of heaths and moors. Nymphs 30mm long usually live in running water in ditches or small streams.

BROWN HAWKER ▷
Aeshna grandis
L 60mm. Widespread and common, especially in southern Europe. Nymphs 40mm long live in ponds and lakes. Adults often feed away from water.

HOW TO WATCH

Adult dragonflies are active fliers and are often seen around ponds and lakes. When they mate, the pair often stay joined together for some time. The female lays her eggs in the water. Sometimes these are dropped onto the surface. Other species insert the eggs into the stem of a water plant. The eggs hatch into nymphs, which eat other pond animals and moult their skins several times. They may take more than one year to reach full size. In the spring, the full-grown nymph leaves the water and climbs a plant stem. The skin splits and the adult dragonfly emerges.

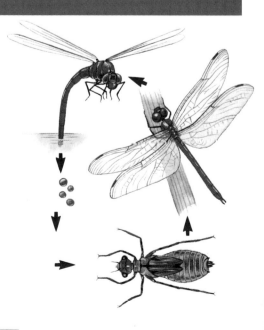

DRAGONFLIES

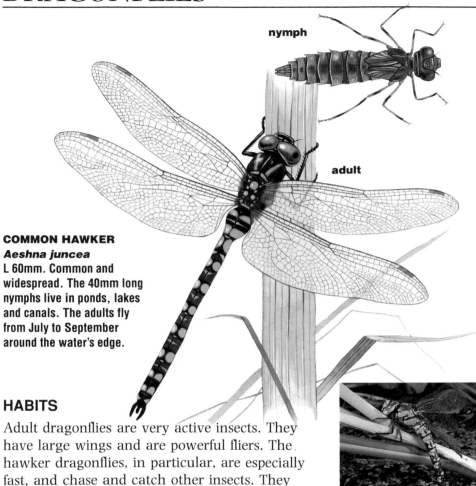

nymph

adult

COMMON HAWKER
Aeshna juncea
L 60mm. Common and
widespread. The 40mm long
nymphs live in ponds, lakes
and canals. The adults fly
from July to September
around the water's edge.

HABITS

Adult dragonflies are very active insects. They
have large wings and are powerful fliers. The
hawker dragonflies, in particular, are especially
fast, and chase and catch other insects. They
often defend a territory around the edge of a
pond and will chase away others of the same
species.

HABITATS

Different species of dragonflies are found in
almost every type of freshwater habitat. Because
they are powerful fliers, they are quick to
colonize new sites. Some species prefer standing
water in ponds, lakes and canals, while a few
are found only in flowing water. Most prefer
well-established habitats with water plants.

Female southern hawker
dragonflies lay their eggs in
the vegetation around the
edge of the pond. Sit quietly
beside a pond in August and
watch carefully. The female
dragonfly will land and crawl
slowly round the pond
margin. When she has found
a suitable site, she arches
her abdomen and lays her
eggs among mosses and
other plants.

SOUTHERN HAWKER
Aeshna cyanea
L 60mm. Common and widespread in the south. Nymphs 40mm long found in ponds and lakes. Adults fly from June to August.

MIGRANT HAWKER ▷
Aeshna mixta
L 50mm Common in the south. In Britain, migrants from the Continent add to the numbers of adults. Nymphs 30mm long.

COMMON DARTER ▲
Sympetrum striolatum
L 40mm. Common and widespread. Nymphs 20mm long live in pools, ponds and lakes. Adults fly from July to October.

PROJECT

In the early summer, dragonflies emerge from their nymphs, usually at dusk. You can sometimes see this in the wild but it is easier to watch at home. Collect a full-grown nymph in the spring and keep it in a tank with weeds and ponds animals for it to eat. Put twigs round the edge for it to climb up and emerge. For a few nights before it emerges, the nymph will search for the best twig.

RUDDY DARTER ▲
Sympetrum sanguineum
L 40mm. A rather localized species. Nymphs live in pools and ponds, sometimes with common darter. Adults fly from July to September.

DRAGONFLIES

DRAGONFLY NYMPHS

Nymphs are the young stages of dragonflies and always live in water. All dragonfly nymphs are carnivorous. They catch pond animals with the special structure called the mask on the underside of their head. Most nymphs live among water plants and stalk their prey. Nymphs of chasers, however, live buried in the silt at the bottom of the pond.

Dragonflies have huge eyes that cover much of the head. Each eye is made up of lots of smaller units called ommatidia. Together, they allow the dragonfly to form an image of the world around it. The eyes are called compound eyes.

DRAGONFLY FEEDING

Adult dragonflies have good eyesight and are powerful fliers. They catch insects such as flies on the wing. Their legs are arranged to form a basket that holds the prey. This is often eaten in flight, or sometimes when the dragonfly returns to its favourite perch. Dragonfly nymphs are also fierce predators.

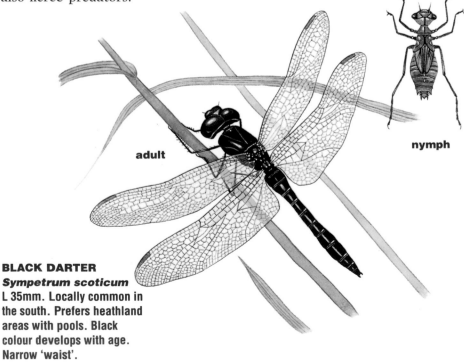

adult

nymph

BLACK DARTER
Sympetrum scoticum
L 35mm. Locally common in the south. Prefers heathland areas with pools. Black colour develops with age. Narrow 'waist'.

BROAD-BODIED CHASER
Libellula depressa
L 45mm. Common in the south. Males are blue, females orange. Flies from May to August. Nymphs 30mm long are found in ponds and lakes.

FOUR-SPOT CHASER ▷
Libellula quadrimaculata
L 45mm. Common and widespread. Wing markings striking. Flies from May to August. Nymphs 30mm long mud-dwellers found in ponds and lakes.

BLACK-LINED SKIMMER ▲
Orthetrum cancellatum
L 40mm. Locally common around pools and lakes. Often in heathland areas. Flies in June and July. Nymphs 30mm long.

KEELED SKIMMER ▲
Orthetrum coerulescens
L 40mm. Locally common especially in the south. On the wing in July and August. Nymphs found in pools and ponds.

PROJECT

After the adult dragonfly has emerged from the nymph it leaves a dry case behind, called the exuvia. Make a collection of the different types by searching around the edge of a pond.

STONEFLIES

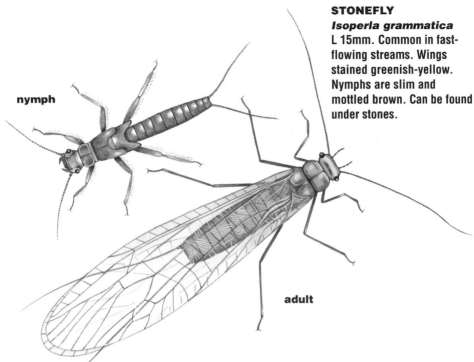

nymph

adult

STONEFLY
Isoperla grammatica
L 15mm. Common in fast-flowing streams. Wings stained greenish-yellow. Nymphs are slim and mottled brown. Can be found under stones.

INTRODUCTION

Stoneflies belong to a group of insects called the Plecoptera. The nymphs live in water and are sensitive to pollution. The adults are very weak fliers and are, consequently, never found far from rivers and lakes. The adults are a favourite food of trout. Not surprisingly, fly fishermen tie artificial flies to imitate them.

GENERAL FEATURES

Adult stoneflies have a flattened appearance with long antennae. Most have two tail appendages. The wings are often slightly hazy. Despite the large wings, they are poor fliers. At rest, the wings are rolled round the body. Male has smaller wings than female. Nymphs have long antennae and two 'tails'. They live at the bottom of lakes and rivers.

At first glance, many of the aquatic stages of insects look alike. Stonefly nymphs can be recognized by the two, long 'tails' at the hind end. The insects are flattened and move by wriggling. Both damselfly and mayfly nymphs have three tail appendages.

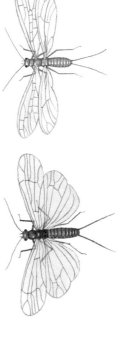

STONEFLY ▷
Chloroperla torrentium
L 8mm. Common in fast-flowing, stony streams. Adults yellowish, seen from April to June. Has distinctive hairy tails.

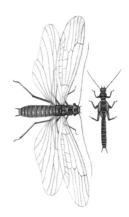

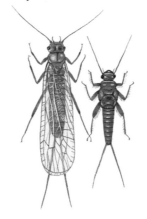

STONEFLY ▲
Leuctra fusca
L 10mm. Lives in fast-flowing streams and rivers. Slender nymphs hide under stones or burrow. Adults seen in May and June.

STONEFLY ▲
Perla bipunctata
L 20mm. Locally common in upland streams and rivers. Adults seen in May and June. Nymphs distinctive brown and yellow.

STONEFLY ▲
Capnia bifrons
L 10mm. Found in fast-flowing streams and around lake shores. Nymphs live in gravel or under stones.

HOW TO WATCH

Although stoneflies are common, they can be rather difficult to find. Adults creep among the waterside plants and seldom fly. They are best found by careful searching. Nymphs often live buried in sand and gravel or under stones. They are found by careful sifting of the sediment. Put some into a white tray and gently sort it with forceps. The nymphs have delicate bodies and are easily damaged. Return them to the water as soon as you have finished with them.

STONEFLIES AND OTHERS

INTRODUCTION

All the animals featured on this page are insects. Two are stoneflies and belong to the group called the Plecoptera. Alderflies look similar but are in fact related to lacewings. *Podura aquatica* is a primitive insect called a springtail. The brown china mark moth is an unusual species whose caterpillar lives in water.

GENERAL FEATURES

The stoneflies have been described on the previous page. Adult alderflies have two pairs of brown wings and slender antennae. The larvae have fierce jaws, seven pairs of feathery gills along the sides of their bodies and a pointed 'tail'. Springtails are aptly named since they can leap large distances for their size.

The young stages of alderflies differ from those of many other water insects such as stoneflies and mayflies. The young stages are very different from the adult and are known as larvae rather than nymphs. There is also a resting stage called the pupa.

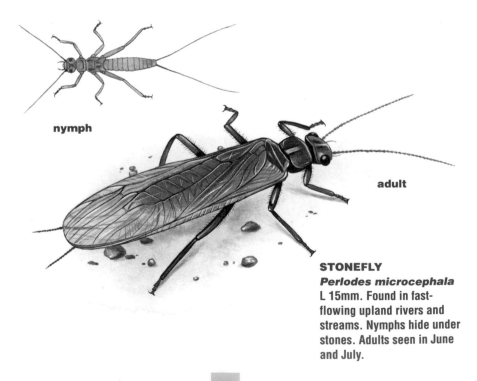

nymph

adult

STONEFLY
Perlodes microcephala
L 15mm. Found in fast-flowing upland rivers and streams. Nymphs hide under stones. Adults seen in June and July.

STONEFLY ▲
Dinocras cephalotes
L 20mm. Locally common in
gently-flowing rivers with
stable sediments. Adults
seen from May to July.

ALDERFLY ▲
Sialis lutaria
L 10mm. Common and
widespread in ponds and
slow-flowing streams. Adults
are poor fliers. Larvae 10mm
long live in silt.

PROJECT

The brown china mark moth has a
caterpillar that lives in water. Look for
small 'tents' made of the leaves of
water lilies and other plants. If you take
one home, you can keep it in an
aquarium until it pupates. The adult
moth will emerge in summer.
Remember to let if go near a pond after
it hatches.

BROWN CHINA MARK ▲
MOTH
Nymphula nymphaeta
L 35mm. Common around
ponds and lakes. Adult flies
from June to August.
Caterpillar makes leaf case.

◀ **SPRINGTAIL**
Podura aquatica
L 2mm. Common on the
surface of ponds and lakes.
When disturbed releases
'spring lever' on underside
of body to escape.

CADDIS FLIES

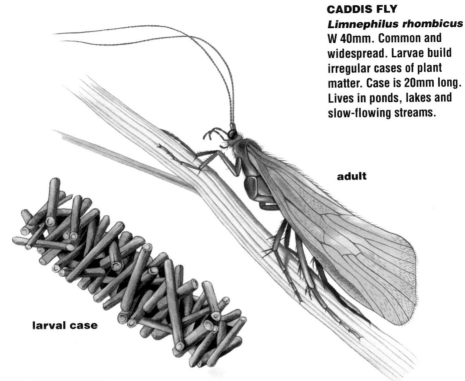

CADDIS FLY
Limnephilus rhombicus
W 40mm. Common and
widespread. Larvae build
irregular cases of plant
matter. Case is 20mm long.
Lives in ponds, lakes and
slow-flowing streams.

adult

larval case

INTRODUCTION

Caddis flies are among the commonest
freshwater insects. There are many different
species. Most people are familiar with the larvae,
which make cases. As adults they are short-
lived. During the daytime they are secretive and
hide among waterside plants. They are easily
disturbed and can be found by careful searching.

HABITATS

Caddis flies are found in most freshwater
habitats. There are many that live in rivers and
streams, but some prefer ponds and lakes. The
larvae are important as food for fish and other
water creatures. Despite their short lives, adults
are also eaten by fish. Fishermen make artificial
flies which resemble them.

At first glance, adult caddis
flies look rather like moths.
The wings of caddis flies are
covered in hairs which can
be seen with a hand lens.
Moth wings, however, are
covered in scales which
make the patterns and
colours.

CADDIS FLY ▽
Phryganea grandis
W 50mm. Found in ponds
and slow-flowing rivers.
Case made from spirally-
arranged leaf portions is
35mm long.

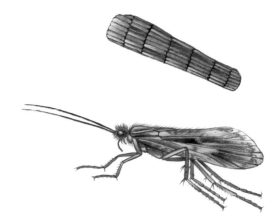

CADDIS FLY △
Limnephilus lunatus
W 25mm. Common in ponds
and streams. Case 20mm
long is made from plant
roots and leaves plus twigs
laid lengthwise.

HOW TO WATCH

Caddis flies have a life-cycle which
has four different stages. These are
called the adult, the eggs, the larva
and the pupa. In the spring, the
female mates and then lays her
eggs underwater. These are often
protected by jelly. In many species,
when the larvae hatch they build
cases in which to live. Some species
have free-living larvae, however.
When fully grown, the larvae
pupate inside a shelter. They hatch
into adults in the spring. The
adults only live for a few days,
while the larvae may live for
many months.

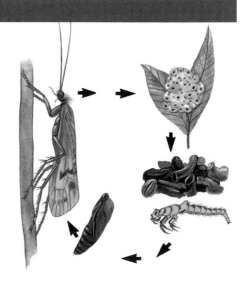

CADDIS FLIES

GENERAL FEATURES

Adult caddis flies are rather moth-like in appearance. They have two pairs of wings which are folded over the body at rest. Unlike moth wings, these are covered with fine hairs. Caddis flies are rather poor fliers, however. They have long antennae which may sometimes be as long as the body itself.

HABITS

Adult caddis flies are not as easy to find as their larvae. During the day they usually hide among the vegetation. If disturbed, they flutter or fly a short distance towards cover. They are most easily seen at dusk. Take a torch, or better still a moth trap, to the edge of a pond and see what species you can attract.

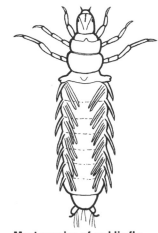

Most species of caddis fly larvae live in cases and move around quite a lot. In order to stay in their cases, the larvae have hooks at the end on the body which grip the inside of their shelter.

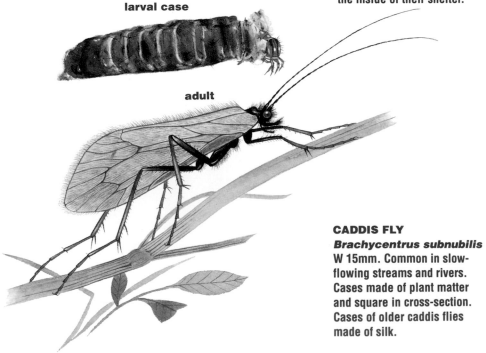

larval case

adult

CADDIS FLY
Brachycentrus subnubilis
W 15mm. Common in slow-flowing streams and rivers. Cases made of plant matter and square in cross-section. Cases of older caddis flies made of silk.

CADDIS FLY
Hydropsyche pelucidula
W 25mm. Common in slow-flowing streams and rivers. Larva spins a silk net rather than making a case. Adult sometimes flies by day.

CADDIS FLY
Agapetus fuscipes
W 15mm. Common in fast-flowing, chalky, stony streams. Case made of small stones. Groups cluster on boulders.

CADDIS FLY
Anabolia nervosa
W 20mm. Common in streams and slow-flowing rivers. Case made of sand with twigs to discourage fish from eating the larvae.

CADDIS FLY
Triaenodes bicolor
W 15mm. Common in still water. Slender case made from spirally-arranged leaf fragments. Larva swims well if disturbed.

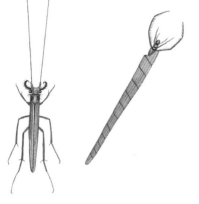

PROJECT

Caddis fly larvae are easily caught by pond dipping. Sometimes they lose their cases. Keep the larva in a tank with plenty of sand, twigs and water plants. It will soon make a new case. Make sure there are no predators in the tank because they will attack it. Do not deliberately remove a larva from its protective case.

CADDIS FLIES

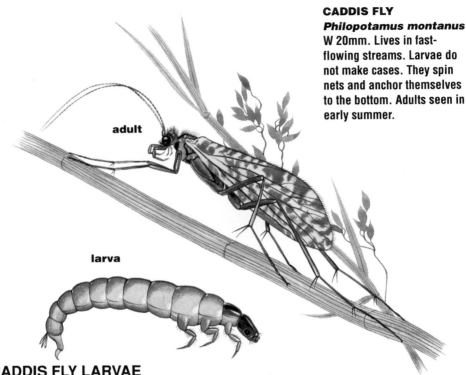

CADDIS FLY
Philopotamus montanus
W 20mm. Lives in fast-flowing streams. Larvae do not make cases. They spin nets and anchor themselves to the bottom. Adults seen in early summer.

adult

larva

CADDIS FLY LARVAE

Caddis fly larvae are easily recognized by the cases that most species make to protect themselves. Depending on the species, these may be built from sand, twigs, leaf fragments or a mixture of all of these materials. Caddis fly larvae are also easy to tell when separated from their cases. Most of the body, except for the head, is soft and grub-like.

HABITS

Those caddis fly larvae that build large cases of twigs and stones usually move in a slow and cumbersome manner. Some species make slender cases and swim freely. Others attach their cases to rocks, and a few live in silk nets rather than cases. Some caddis fly larvae eat only plant material, others are carnivorous.

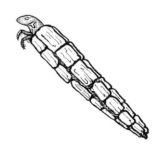

Only the head, thorax and legs of the caddis fly larvae protrude from its case. These have a hard outer coating to protect them. Inside the case, the body is soft.

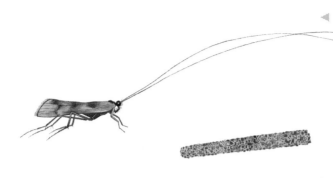

CADDIS FLY
Mystacides longicornis
W 20mm. Lives in still water, especially ponds. Case made from sand and gravel. Adult wings distinctively marked.

CADDIS FLY ▶
Micropterna sequax
W 30mm. Common in fast-flowing streams. Case made from sand and gravel. Adult seen from June to August.

CADDIS FLY
Halesus radiatus
W 35mm. Lives in rivers and streams. Case made from plant material with twigs running lengthwise. Adults fly in the autumn.

CADDIS FLY ▶
Sericostoma personatum
W 30mm. Common in streams. Case made from small grains of sand and curved slightly. Adults seen in late summer.

MAYFLIES

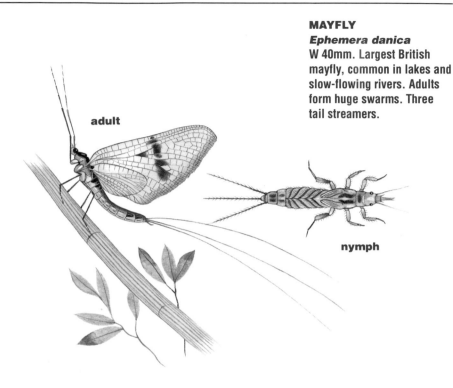

MAYFLY
Ephemera danica
W 40mm. Largest British mayfly, common in lakes and slow-flowing rivers. Adults form huge swarms. Three tail streamers.

adult

nymph

INTRODUCTION

Mayflies are common freshwater insects. They belong to a group called the Ephemeroptera. The young stages are called nymphs. Because they live for a year or more, they can be found in water at any season. The adults only live for a few hours or days. As their name suggests, most species emerge in late May.

GENERAL FEATURES

Adult mayflies can be easily recognized. They have two pairs of wings. The front pair is much larger than the hind pair. They also have two, or sometimes three, long 'tails'. Adults have very short antennae. Mayfly nymphs have slender bodies with three tails. There are pairs of feathery gills along the side of the body.

Mayfly nymphs can breathe oxygen dissolved in water. They have seven pairs of feathery gills along the side of the abdomen. The nymphs are very sensitive to pollution. Most species are found in clean, flowing water.

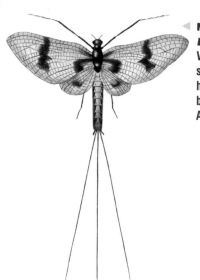

MAYFLY ◀
Ephemera vulgata
W 40mm. Locally common in slow-flowing rivers. Nymphs have elongated head and burrow in sand and mud. Adults fly in June.

MAYFLY ▼
Baetis rhodani
W 20mm. Common in fast-flowing streams. Adult has small hind wings and two tail streamers. Flies in spring and summer.

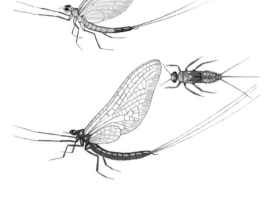

MAYFLY ▶
Ephemerella ignita
W 20mm. Common in fast-flowing streams. Nymphs found on stones and swim well. Adults have three tail streamers.

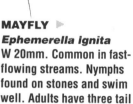

HOW TO WATCH

In many species of mayfly, the adults all emerge at roughly the same time. This is called synchronized hatching. This usually occurs in late May or early June. The males form large swarms which fly up and down over the water. Swarming usually occurs on warm evenings. Visit a likely-looking river when the weather and time of year are suitable. Arrive half an hour or so before sunset and watch for the insects. If a female flies into the swarm, she is immediately grabbed by a male and mating takes place in flight.

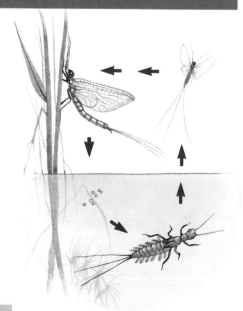

MAYFLIES

HABITS

Adult mayflies are very short-lived creatures. Some live for less than a day. During the day, they usually rest among the waterside vegetation. They hold their wings folded vertically over their bodies. The nymphs always live in water. Many species burrow in the sand or mud, but a few are free-living.

HABITATS

Mayflies are found in most types of freshwater habitat except where the water is stagnant. Most species, however, are found in flowing water because the nymphs have to breathe dissolved oxygen. They soon die if removed from the water into a sampling bottle. They are also very easily killed by pollution.

Mayflies are the only group of insects that have wings before they become adults. In the spring, the nymph emerges from the water and a stage called the sub-imago hatches. The adult emerges from it shortly afterwards.

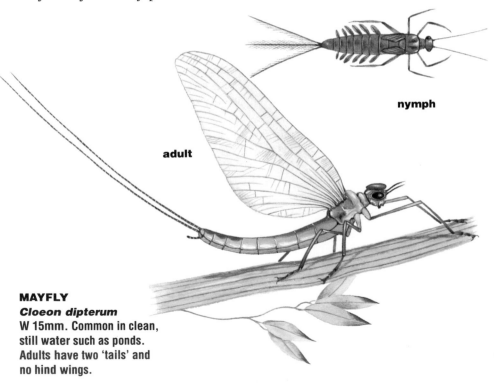

nymph

adult

MAYFLY
Cloeon dipterum
W 15mm. Common in clean, still water such as ponds. Adults have two 'tails' and no hind wings.

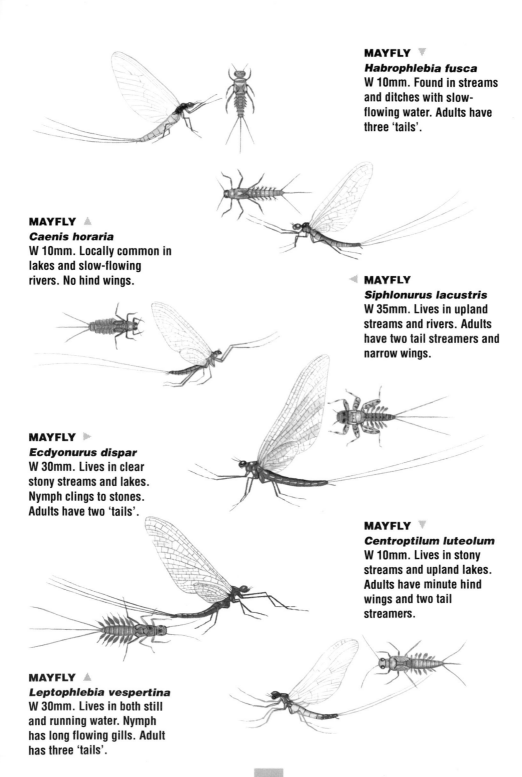

MAYFLY ▽
Habrophlebia fusca
W 10mm. Found in streams
and ditches with slow-
flowing water. Adults have
three 'tails'.

MAYFLY ▲
Caenis horaria
W 10mm. Locally common in
lakes and slow-flowing
rivers. No hind wings.

◁ MAYFLY
Siphlonurus lacustris
W 35mm. Lives in upland
streams and rivers. Adults
have two tail streamers and
narrow wings.

MAYFLY ▷
Ecdyonurus dispar
W 30mm. Lives in clear
stony streams and lakes.
Nymph clings to stones.
Adults have two 'tails'.

MAYFLY ▽
Centroptilum luteolum
W 10mm. Lives in stony
streams and upland lakes.
Adults have minute hind
wings and two tail
streamers.

MAYFLY ▲
Leptophlebia vespertina
W 30mm. Lives in both still
and running water. Nymph
has long flowing gills. Adult
has three 'tails'.

WATER BUGS

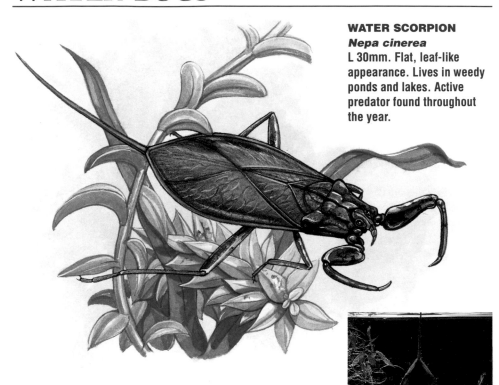

INTRODUCTION

Water scorpions and their relatives are all water bugs. They belong to a group of insects called Hemiptera. Some water bugs live in the water while others live on the surface. Most species have papery wings that are folded over the body when the insect is resting.

GENERAL FEATURES

Water bugs have sharp, pointed mouthparts. Many species are predators and use these to pierce their prey. Water bugs do not have gills. In order to breathe, those species that live in the water have to collect air from the surface. Some have a breathing tube while others carry a bubble of air with them. Eggs are laid in the stems and leaves of waterplants.

Place a water scorpion in a jar of pondwater with some weed. It will crawl around among the plants. Occasionally it will walk backwards towards the surface. It breaks the surface film with the long thin breathing tube in its tail to collect fresh air.

WATER MEASURER ▷
Hydrometra stagnorum
L 10mm. Common on ponds,
ditches and slow-flowing
river margins. Walks slowly
over the surface. Long,
slender body.

POND SKATER ▲
Gerris lacustris
L 10mm. Common on ponds
and lakes. Skates over the
surface. Feeds on insects
trapped in the surface film.

WATER STICK INSECT ▷
Ranatra linearis
L 50mm. Lives in shallow
ponds and lakes among
water plants. Motionless for
long periods. Occasionally
leaves the water and flies.

PROJECT

Some pond animals are active and easy
to see when caught in a pond net.
However, some keep still and may look
like pieces of plants. These are more
difficult to spot. The best way to find
them is to put your net sample in a tray
and just wait. Once things have settled
down after a few minutes, the animals
will begin to slowly move. The
photograph above shows a water stick
insect eating a water shrimp.

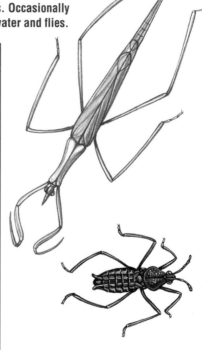

WATER CRICKET ▲
Velia caprai
L 7.5mm. Lives on ponds,
woodland pools and slow-
flowing streams. Usually
wingless with thick body.

WATER BUGS

HABITATS

Water bugs are found in all sorts of different types of freshwater habitats. They all breathe air and have to return to the surface of the water from time to time. Ponds and lakes are the best habitats for water bugs. Only a few species live in streams and rivers except where the current is slow-flowing.

HABITS

Although some water bugs feed on plant matter, most are predators. They use their mouthparts to feed. Be careful if you are handling them in a net. The water boatman and other species can pierce human skin and cause a painful bite. Some water bugs readily leave the water in warm weather, and can fly quite well.

Place a needle on paper in some water. As the paper sinks, the needle floats, showing surface tension. This same process allows the water boatman to 'walk' on water. It uses its legs like oars to swim.

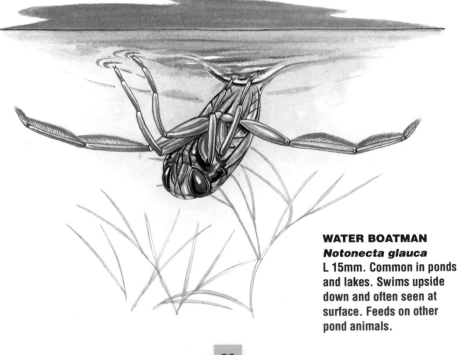

WATER BOATMAN
Notonecta glauca
L 15mm. Common in ponds and lakes. Swims upside down and often seen at surface. Feeds on other pond animals.

LESSER WATER BOATMAN
Corixa punctata
L 10mm. Common in ponds and lakes. Swims the right way up. Feeds on plant matter on the pond bed.

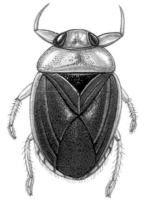

SAUCER BUG ▷
Ilyocoris cimicoides
L 10mm. Lives in overgrown ponds and lakes. Predatory and can give painful bite. Feeds on other small water insects.

WATER BUG ◣
Plea atomaria
L 5mm. Lives among vegetation in still ponds and lakes. Feeds on small crustaceans.

WATER BUG ▷
Cymatia coleoptera
L 3mm. Locally common in ponds and shallow lakes. Hides among weeds. Feeds on small pond animals.

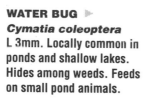

HOW TO WATCH

The saucer bug is a large, flattened bug that lives in weedy ponds and lakes. If you keep one in a tank, you will be able to see how it breathes. The underside of its body is covered in a silvery film. This is a layer of air which provides the animal with oxygen. Air is also held underneath the wings. From time to time, the saucer bug returns to the surface of the water to replace its air supply, increasing if the animal is active or warm.

WATER BEETLES

WATER BEETLE
Platambus maculatus
L 7mm. Lives in streams and rivers among vegetation. Recognized by distinctive markings. Seen during summer months.

INTRODUCTION

Beetles belong to a group of insects called the Coleoptera. They are one of the easiest groups to recognize. Adult beetles have hard, shiny bodies and are usually very active creatures. Beetles are extremely numerous insects. There are more than 4,000 species in this group. Over 100 of these live in water all the time and are called water beetles.

GENERAL FEATURES

Adult beetles have two pairs of wings like other insects. However, the front pair are hardened. They form a hard case called the elytra which protects the hind wings. This is their most distinctive feature. At rest, the wings are usually folded beneath the elytra. Most water beetles can fly, although they spend much of their lives in water.

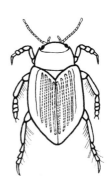

The third pair of legs in many species of water beetles (the hind legs) is flattened and fringed with stiff hairs. This enables the beetle to swim better in the water. The other legs are less important in swimming.

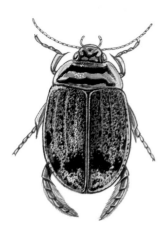

WATER BEETLE
Acilius sulcatus
L 20mm. Common and widespread in ponds and lakes. Wing cases have beautiful markings. Those of male are smooth. Wing cases of female are ribbed.

WATER BEETLE ▷
Hydroporus palustris
L 5mm. Common and widespread in ponds and lakes. Variable orange pattern on wing cases. Seen at most times of year. Lives among water plants.

WATER BEETLE
Ilybius fenestratus
L 11mm. Common in ponds and lakes. Sometimes also in slow-flowing streams. Black body has reddish tint. Keeps to the bottom layers.

SCREECH BEETLE ▷
Hygrobia hermanni
L 13mm. Common and widespread in ponds and ditches. Lives among water plants. When disturbed, it squeaks loudly by rubbing its body against its wing cases.

WATER BEETLES

LIFE-CYCLES

Water beetles have four very different stages in their life-cycles. These are the adult, the egg, the larva and the pupa. Adult water beetles mate and the female lays eggs in the water. The larvae hatch from these and take several months to become fully grown. In most species, the larva leaves the water and burrows into the ground to pupate.

LIFE IN WATER

Water beetles have several features which suit them to a life in water. Species that are active swimmers usually have a streamlined body and legs that help them swim. Adult water beetles breathe air and must return to the water's surface from time to time. They keep a supply of air beneath the wing case and, in some species, under the body.

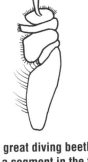

Male great diving beetles have a segment in the front leg which is swollen and flattened. This is used to grip the female when mating.

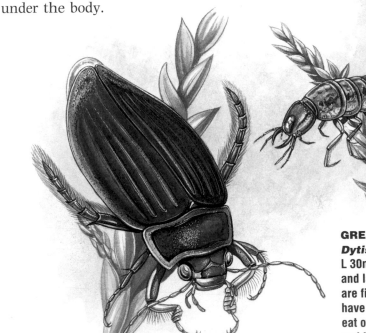

GREAT DIVING BEETLE
Dytiscus marginalis
L 30mm. Common in ponds and lakes. Adults and larvae are fierce predators. Larvae have large mandibles. Both eat other insects, tadpoles and fish.

WATER BEETLE
Haliplus fulvus
L 5mm. Common in over-grown ponds and ditches. Crawls among weeds instead of swimming. Feeds on plant matter.

WATER BEETLE
Laccobius sinuatus
L 4mm. Common and widespread in ponds, slow-flowing streams and weedy ditches. A poor swimmer.

WATER BEETLE
Hydrobius fuscipes
L 8mm. Common and widespread in ponds and ditches. Body extremely shiny. Reddish legs. Grub-like larva.

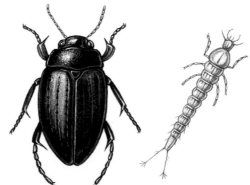

WATER BEETLE
Agabus bipustulatus
L 10mm. Common and widespread in ponds, lakes and ditches. Crawls among water plants and on the bottom instead of swimming.

WATER BEETLES

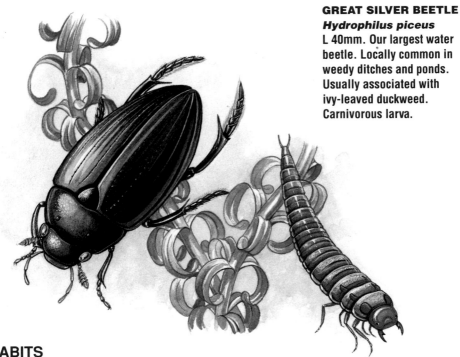

GREAT SILVER BEETLE
Hydrophilus piceus
L 40mm. Our largest water beetle. Locally common in weedy ditches and ponds. Usually associated with ivy-leaved duckweed. Carnivorous larva.

HABITS

Water beetles spend most if not all of their lives in water. Not surprisingly, many of them can swim well. They have powerful hind legs and are streamlined. Some, however, crawl among the weeds instead of swimming. Most water beetle adults and larvae are carnivorous. Some, such as the great diving beetle, catch prey such as small fish.

HABITATS

Water beetles are found in almost all types of freshwater habitats. Ponds and lakes are particularly rich hunting grounds and pools or ditches on heathland have many interesting species. Some even live in brackish pools by the sea. Because many water beetles can fly actively in warm weather, they are quick to colonize new habitats.

Adult great silver beetles are vegetarians. Their larvae, however, are predators. They have powerful jaws with which they eat water snails and other aquatic animals.

WATER BEETLE
Helophorus aquaticus
L 7mm. Locally common in weedy ponds. Usually found at the water's edge. Ridged thorax is characteristic.

WATER BEETLE ▶
Elmis aenea
L 2mm. Lives in fast-flowing streams. Crawls under stones and across the bottom of the stream. Feeds on water plants.

WATER BEETLE
Laccophilus minutus
L 5mm. Fairly common in southern Britain. Lives in overgrown ponds, lakes and ditches. Flattened body. Swims actively.

PROJECT

Adult water beetles have to breathe air. They do not have gills. Many have a supply of air beneath their wing cases or under the body which they renew from time to time. Watch a beetle in a tank. Some species come to the surface tail-first, while a few come to the surface head first. Count the number of times a beetle will visit the surface in an hour.

▲ WHIRLYGIG BEETLE
Gyrinus natator
L 6mm. Common in ponds and still water. Large groups often seen whirling on surface. Dive if disturbed. Middle and hind legs short.

MOSQUITOES AND RELATIVES

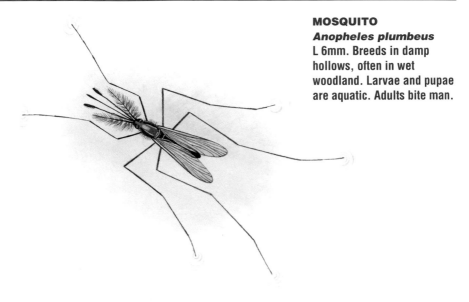

MOSQUITO
Anopheles plumbeus
L 6mm. Breeds in damp
hollows, often in wet
woodland. Larvae and pupae
are aquatic. Adults bite man.

INTRODUCTION

Mosquitoes belong to a group of insects that are
called true flies, or Diptera. This word literally
means 'two wings'. It reflects the fact that most
species fly using only one pair of wings. Adult
diptera are terrestrial although most mosquitoes
and gnats are found near fresh water. Their
eggs, larvae and pupae are aquatic.

GENERAL FEATURES

Although mosquitoes and other true flies do
have two pairs of wings, they only use one to
fly. The second pair is much reduced in size.
They help the insect balance in flight. When
flying, mosquitoes make a whining or buzzing
sound caused by their wings beating. Most have
sharp mouthparts and many feed on blood.

Mosquito pupae float at the
surface of the water. They
hatch into adults directly
from the water. Keep a few in
a jar and watch the process.
First the skin of the pupa
splits and then the mosquito
pulls itself onto the surface
film of the water.

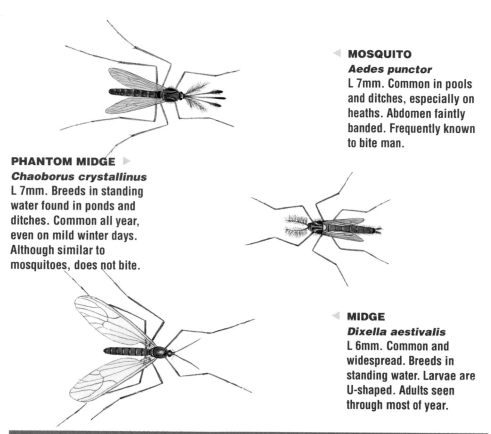

MOSQUITO
Aedes punctor
L 7mm. Common in pools
and ditches, especially on
heaths. Abdomen faintly
banded. Frequently known
to bite man.

PHANTOM MIDGE ▷
Chaoborus crystallinus
L 7mm. Breeds in standing
water found in ponds and
ditches. Common all year,
even on mild winter days.
Although similar to
mosquitoes, does not bite.

MIDGE
Dixella aestivalis
L 6mm. Common and
widespread. Breeds in
standing water. Larvae are
U-shaped. Adults seen
through most of year.

HOW TO WATCH

There are four stages in the life-
cycle of mosquitoes and all true
flies. The stages are the adult, egg,
larva and pupa. Adult mosquitoes
are terrestrial and fly well. After
mating, the female lays her eggs on
the water. In many species, the
female has to feed on blood to lay
her eggs successfully. The young
larvae breathe air, so they float to
the surface after hatching. They
have a breathing siphon to help
them. If disturbed, they swim to
the bottom with a wriggling
motion. When fully grown, they
turn into pupae from which the
adults hatch.

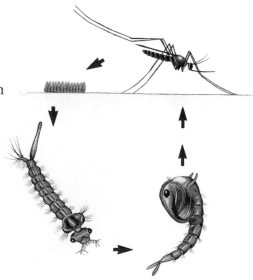

GNATS, SPIDERS AND OTHERS

INTRODUCTION

Gnats, blackfly and rat-tailed maggots are all insects and belong to a group called the Diptera or true flies. Spiders and mites, on the other hand, are not insects, but belong to a group of animals called the Arachnids. The water spider is the only spider in this group that spends its entire life underwater.

The water spider has a silvery appearance underwater. This is due to a layer of air that it traps round its body. It builds a silk tent in which a bubble of air is trapped. The spider uses this air to breathe underwater.

GENERAL FEATURES

Like other flies, those on this page have three pairs of legs and fly using one pair of wings. The second pair are reduced in size. Spiders and water mites have four pairs of legs and no wings. There are many different species of water mites found in rivers and ponds. Many of them are brightly coloured.

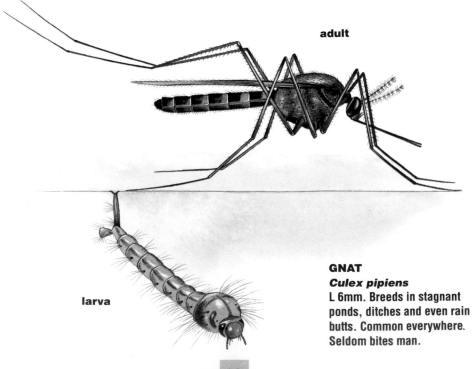

adult

larva

GNAT
Culex pipiens
L 6mm. Breeds in stagnant ponds, ditches and even rain butts. Common everywhere. Seldom bites man.

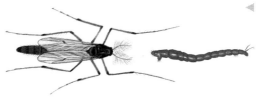

CHIRONOMID MIDGE
Chironomus plumosus
L 8mm. Breeds in stagnant ponds and pools. Larvae, known as bloodworms, are bright red. Live in bottom sediments.

BLACKFLY ▶
Simulium equinum
L 3mm. Breeds in fast-flowing streams in upland areas. Larvae are attached to stones. Adult female sucks blood.

RAT-TAILED MAGGOT
Eristalis tenax
L 12mm. Also known as a drone fly. Larvae found in stagnant pools. Long breathing siphon at tail end. Adults resemble drone honey bees. Frequently hover.

WATER MITE ▲
Hydrarachna globosa
L 2mm. Common in ponds. Adults are free living and bright red. The larvae are duller and are the parasites of water bugs.

WATER SPIDER
Argyroneta aquatica
L 12mm. Britain's only aquatic spider. Locally common in clean, weed-filled ponds and ditches. Builds webs underwater to trap air for breathing.

RAFT SPIDER ▲

Dolomedes fimbriatus
L 40mm. Local at heathland pools. Catches aquatic animals and insects trapped in surface film. Dives and swims well if disturbed.

WATER SNAILS

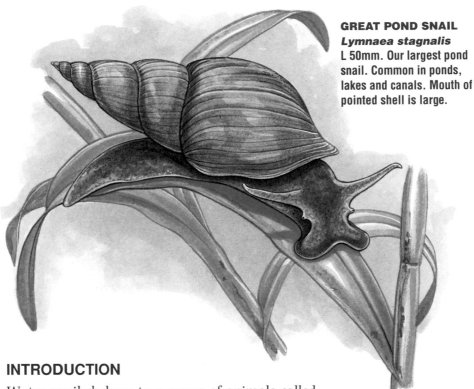

GREAT POND SNAIL
Lymnaea stagnalis
L 50mm. Our largest pond
snail. Common in ponds,
lakes and canals. Mouth of
pointed shell is large.

INTRODUCTION

Water snails belong to a group of animals called
the Molluscs. Freshwater limpets and mussels
are also members of this group. The main
characteristic of these animals is that they have
a hard shell. This protects their soft body. They
use calcium in the water in chalky areas to
make the shell. Not surprisingly, few molluscs
are found in water with little calcium.

GENERAL FEATURES

Water snails live inside a shell which is
arranged in a spiral in most species. In some
kinds, such as the ramshorn snails, the shell is
flattened, while it is pointed in the pond snails.
Freshwater mussels, which are relatives of the
water snails, have shells divided into two halves.
The soft body is found between the two.

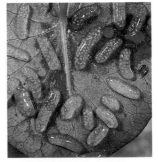

Great pond snails lay their
eggs in sausage-shaped
masses of jelly. These can
often be found underneath
water lily leaves in the
summer. The jelly protects
the young snails.

WANDERING SNAIL
Lymnaea pereger
L 12mm. Common and widespread in ponds, lakes and ditches. Mouth of shell is large in relation to the

DWARF POND SNAIL ▷
Lymnaea truncatula
L 8mm. Common at the edges of streams and ditches and in trampled, marshy ground.

EARED POND SNAIL
Lymnaea auricularia
L 20mm. Common in chalk-rich ponds and lakes. Mouth of shell large and ear-shaped. Not found during summer months.

MARSH SNAIL ▷
Lymnaea palustris
L 20mm. Locally distributed in marshes and drainage ditches. Shell is narrowly pointed with small opening.

COMMON BITHYNIA
Bithynia tentaculata
L 12mm. Common in canals, lakes and rivers. A hard plate – the operculum – closes mouth of shell when body withdraws.

WATER SNAILS

HABITATS

Water snails live in all sorts of different
freshwater habitats. Only a few species live in
heathland areas, most preferring a chalky
habitat. Some water snails and their relatives
can only live in flowing water where there is
plenty of oxygen. However, many species live in
ponds and lakes.

LIFE IN WATER

Some types of snails have gills. These help them
take up oxygen which is dissolved in the water.
They do not have to come to the surface to
breathe air. Other snails have a chamber inside
the shell which holds air. They use this to
breathe underwater. These snails have to come
to the surface from time to time to replace air.

Operculate snails are those
with a plate, or operculum,
which closes the mouth of
the shell. When they are
moving, the operculum can
be seen attached to the foot.

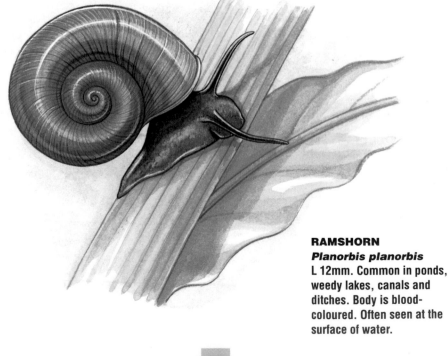

RAMSHORN
Planorbis planorbis
L 12mm. Common in ponds,
weedy lakes, canals and
ditches. Body is blood-
coloured. Often seen at the
surface of water.

FRESHWATER WINKLE
Viviparus viviparus
L 35mm. Locally common in slow-flowing rivers. Shell has distinctive markings and operculum is prominent.

JENKIN'S SPIRE SHELL
Potamopyrgus jenkinsii
L 5mm. Small, increasingly widespread in rivers and streams. Has spread inland from brackish water.

KEELED RAMSHORN
Planorbis carinatus
L 15mm. Common in chalky ponds and lakes. Distinct keel runs round shell when viewed from the side.

WHIRLPOOL RAMSHORN
Planorbis vortex
L 10mm. Common in chalky rivers and streams, but sometimes in ponds. Shell has tight whorls and is flattened on one side.

FLAT RAMSHORN
Planorbis complanatus
L 5mm. Common in ponds and weedy lakes. Shell flattened on one side with large whorls. No keel or ridge seen in side view.

WATER SNAILS

HABITS

Water snails move using a muscular foot. Large numbers of small hairs on the underside of the foot beat in the same direction. This enables the animal to move. Water snails have two tentacles at the head end. These detect the environment around the animal. There are also simple eyes at the head end. They are usually near the base of the tentacles.

Planorbid snails carry a cavity full of air inside the shell. This enables them to breathe underwater. They also have a pigment in their blood which colours it red like our own. This carries oxygen around the body, and helps them to live in stagnant water.

FEEDING

Most water snails feed using their tongue, which is called a radula. This has a rough surface covered with minute teeth. It is used to rasp algae growing on the surface of plants and to cut pieces of leaves. Most water snails have both male and female organs. Although they can fertilise themselves, they usually mate with another snail.

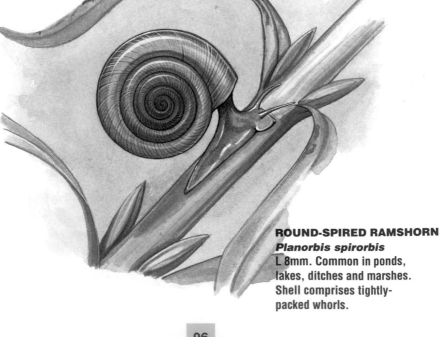

ROUND-SPIRED RAMSHORN
Planorbis spirorbis
L 8mm. Common in ponds, lakes, ditches and marshes. Shell comprises tightly-packed whorls.

GREAT RAMSHORN
Planorbarius corneus
L 30mm. Common in chalky ponds and canals. The largest species of ramshorn. Lays eggs in long masses on plants and stones.

BLADDER SNAIL ▶
Physa fontinalis
L 10mm. Common in clean, flowing water. Shell extremely soft and partly covered by body tissue projections when the animal is extended.

VALVE SNAIL
Valvata piscinalis
L 6mm. Common in gently flowing rivers and streams. Head has pronounced snout and long tentacles.

HOW TO WATCH

Fill three identical jars with pond water. Place some ramshorn snails in one, great pond snails in another, and common bithynias in the third. Keep a record of how many times the snails in each jar come to the surface for air. The great pond snails will come to the surface most frequently to collect air. Ramshorn snails can store oxygen. They do not have to come to the surface as often. The common bithynias breathe using gills which remove oxygen dissolved in the water. They do not have to come to the surface for air at all.

LIMPETS AND MUSSELS

RIVER LIMPET
Ancylus fluviatile
L 9mm. Common in fast-flowing water such as streams and rivers. Shell found attached to stones and plants.

GENERAL FEATURES

Not all freshwater molluscs have spiral shells. The river limpet and the lake limpet have conical shells with a hooked tip. Orb shells, pea mussels and zebra mussels have shells in two halves. When the animal is disturbed, they close together tightly to protect the soft body inside.

HABITS

River and lake limpets are well named because they live in rivers and lakes respectively. They are usually found on stones and boulders, and clamp their shell close to the rock when they are not feeding or moving. Orb shells and pea mussels live half buried in silt. Zebra mussels attach themselves to objects in the water.

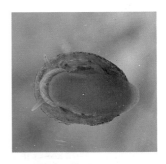

Freshwater limpets are difficult to watch closely. Most of their body is covered by the shell. Gently place one on a small piece of glass in water. When the animal has gripped the glass, turn it over and look at the head, tentacles and foot.

ORB SHELL ▽
Sphaerium corneum
L 10mm. Common in silt at the bottom of ponds, lakes and slow-flowing streams. Shell is very round when it is closed.

▲ LAKE LIMPET
Ancylus lacustris
L 5mm. Common on water plants in lakes and ponds. Hooked tip of flattened shell is twisted to the left.

PROJECT

Place a few orb shells in a tank with silt and gravel at the bottom. They will soon start to partly bury themselves in the sediment using their foot. Eventually, two siphon tubes will appear from between the two halves of the shell. One sucks in water while the other pumps it out. Filters inside the animal remove particles of food.

PEA MUSSEL ▲
Pisidium spp.
L 10mm. Common in silt on the bottom of ponds and rivers. Like *Sphaerium*, a muscular foot helps the animal move.

ZEBRA MUSSEL ▲
Dreissena polymorpha
L 20mm. Striped pattern on shell. Groups found attached to underwater objects in reservoirs and slow rivers.

MUSSELS

GENERAL FEATURES

The freshwater mussels on this page are molluscs and related to the water snails. Because their shells are divided into two halves, they are called bivalves. The shell protects the soft body of the animal. A powerful foot enables the animal to change its position. Water is sucked in, and oxygen and food are filtered out, inside the body.

HABITS

Freshwater mussels do not move around like water snails. They spend most of their lives with their shells partly embedded in sediment at the bottom of lakes and rivers. When disturbed, the mussel can clamp the two halves of its shell tightly together. Most of the time, however, the shell is partly open.

Like water snails, the shells of freshwater mussels get bigger as they grow older. They are held together by a hinge. Near the hinge is hump called the umbo. This is the oldest part of the shell. New shell grows around the umbo year by year.

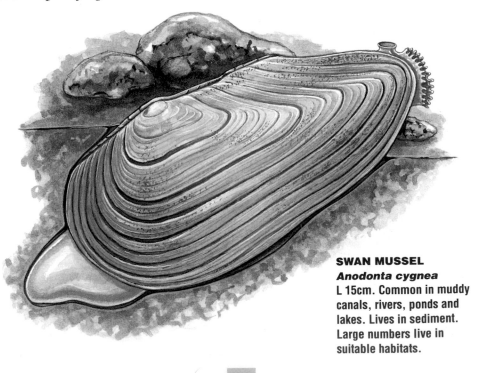

SWAN MUSSEL
Anodonta cygnea
L 15cm. Common in muddy canals, rivers, ponds and lakes. Lives in sediment. Large numbers live in suitable habitats.

PEARL MUSSEL
Margaritifera margaritifera
L 10cm. Locally common in fast-flowing rivers in north and west. Pearls produced to coat irritating foreign particles which enter the shell.

PAINTER'S MUSSEL ▷
Unio pictorum
L 10cm. Locally common in ponds, lakes, canals and slow rivers in the south. Three 'teeth' can be seen along the hinge.

DUCK MUSSEL
Anodonta anatina
L 10cm. Locally common in sandy rivers and streams. Lives in sediment. Shell more oval shape than the swan mussel.

PROJECT

Duck mussels breathe and feed by sucking in water through a siphon and filtering out oxygen and particles of food. The water is passed out through a second siphon. To watch a mussel feed, put one in a tank of water. Leave it to settle and relax the two halves of its shell. You will see two siphons appear. With a pipette, take up some of the fine sediment from the bottom of the tank. Allow it to trickle towards the siphons. Some of the material will be drawn into the body of the mussel. After a short while, the particles will be seen emerging from the other siphon in a jet of water.

FISH

BROOK LAMPREY
Lampetra planeri
L 14cm. Lives in fast-flowing streams. Sucker is used to hold on to stones. They gather in groups to spawn in the spring.

HABITAT

Fish are found in many different freshwater habitats. Because they breathe oxygen dissolved in the water, most species cannot live in stagnant water. Brook lampreys, bullheads and brown trout live in clear, fast-flowing streams. Salmon move up rivers from the sea to breed, while common eels can be found in a great variety of habitats.

HABITS

Although a few freshwater fish eat plant matter, most species eat pond animals including other fish. Young brook lampreys filter small animals from the water. As adults, they do not feed at all. Bullheads, brook lampreys and brown trout do not move very far during their lives. Salmon, however, migrate hundreds of miles.

There are several different species of lampreys. Most feed by sucking the blood of other fishes. However, the adult brook lamprey does not feed. It uses its sucker to hold on to the stream bed so that it does not get washed away by the current.

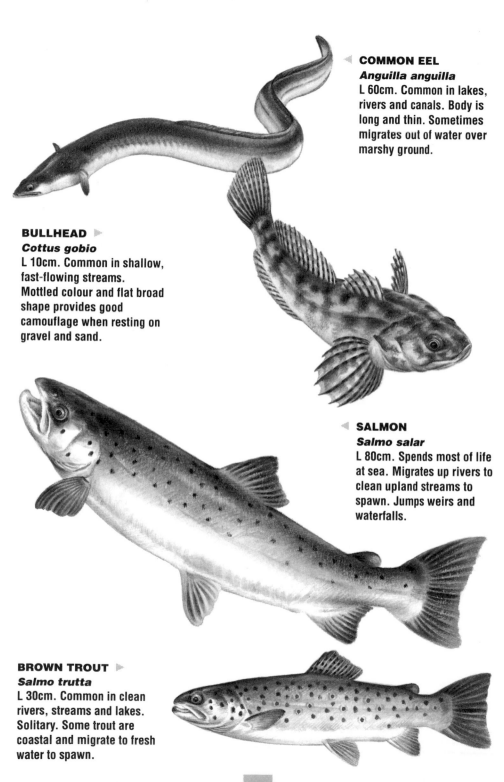

COMMON EEL
Anguilla anguilla
L 60cm. Common in lakes, rivers and canals. Body is long and thin. Sometimes migrates out of water over marshy ground.

BULLHEAD ▷
Cottus gobio
L 10cm. Common in shallow, fast-flowing streams. Mottled colour and flat broad shape provides good camouflage when resting on gravel and sand.

SALMON
Salmo salar
L 80cm. Spends most of life at sea. Migrates up rivers to clean upland streams to spawn. Jumps weirs and waterfalls.

BROWN TROUT ▷
Salmo trutta
L 30cm. Common in clean rivers, streams and lakes. Solitary. Some trout are coastal and migrate to fresh water to spawn.

FISH

HABITAT

Minnows live in upland lakes and in rivers with a good flow of water. However, the other fish on this page prefer lowland lakes and slow-flowing rivers with a lush growth of water plants. This provides them with good spawning and feeding grounds. Gudgeon, carp and tench feed mostly among the bottom sediments, eating many freshwater animals.

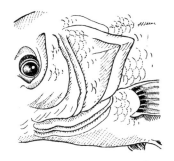

HABITS

Some fish, such as the gudgeon, are mainly solitary and live on their own. Others, such as the tench and the carp, come together in the spring and form what are called shoals. These can sometimes be seen in shallow water. Minnows and small chub spend most of their lives in schools, however. They find safety in numbers from predators.

Fish use gills to take up oxygen dissolved in the water. The gills are at the back of the head. They are full of blood vessels and are arranged in rows. When the fish takes a mouthful of water, it is forced backwards over the gills. It leaves the mouth through gill openings on the sides of the head.

GUDGEON
Gobio gobio
L 12cm. Common in lakes and rivers. A barbel, or fleshy thread, at each side of the mouth helps to sense food. Lives mostly on the bottom. Spawns in shallows.

TENCH
Tinca tinca
L 50cm. Locally common in lakes and slow-flowing rivers. Beautiful olive and golden colour. Feeds on freshwater animals.

CARP ▷
Cyprinus carpio
L 70cm. Common in slow-flowing rivers and lakes. Feeds on algae and worms at the bottom. Spawns in shallows in early summer. Scales absent in some individuals.

CHUB
Leuciscus cephalus
L 30cm. Found mostly in rivers, sometimes in lakes. Orange anal fin. Young form shoals. Spawns in shallow, flowing water.

MINNOW ▷
Phoxinus phoxinus
L 8cm. Common in stony pollution-free rivers and lakes. Males develop red belly in breeding season. Spawn over gravel in spring.

FISH

DACE
Leuciscus leuciscus
L 15cm. Common and
widespread. Scales large in
relation to size of body. Body
rather slim. Anal and
pectoral fins yellowish.

HABITATS

All the fish shown on these pages are related to
the carp. They prefer to live in slow-flowing
rivers and in large lakes. In rivers, they like
areas such as backwaters where the current is
weak and where there is a good growth of
water plants. Fallen trees and branches provide
shelter from predators both in rivers and lakes.

HABITS

Dace, rudd, roach and bream are all found in
shoals. These can be made up of anything from
10 to 100 fish. Living in a shoal provides some
protection from predators. There are more pairs
of eyes to look out for danger. All four species of
fish feed on a mixture of plant material and
small animals such as insect larvae and snails.

The body of almost all fish is
covered in prominent scales.
These overlap each other
and protect the skin beneath.
Scales grow with the fish.
The age of a fish can be told
by the number of annual
growth rings on the scales.

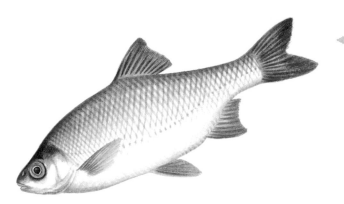

ROACH
Rutilus rutilus
L 30cm. Common and widespread. Silvery scales and red eyes. Dorsal fin lies over pelvic fins. Feeds on plants and animals.

RUDD ▷
Scardinius erythrophthalmus
L 25cm. Common, especially in the south. Scales large with golden tint. Dorsal fin lies behind pelvic fins.

PROJECT

Bleak are members of the carp family. They are often found in slow-flowing lowland rivers. In the spring, large shoals move into shallow areas of gravel and sand where they lay their eggs. Sit quietly beside the bank and watch them spawn. Try to work out which are males and which are females by their behaviour. A shoal may contain several hundred bleak.

BREAM
Abramis brama
L 30cm. Locally common. Body is flat and deep. Scales small with golden bronze colour. Spawns among weed-filled water.

FISH

HABITAT

Pike and perch are large fish that live in slow-flowing rivers, lakes and gravel pits. They are often found among the weedy margins, but also swim in open, deep water. Three-spined and nine-spined sticklebacks live in many different freshwater habitats, from lakes and ponds, to rivers and streams. They can also be found in seawater.

Fish swim using fins. The tail fin gives the fish power. The other fins control its movement. There is a dorsal fin – two in some species – an anal fin, two pectoral fins behind the gill openings and two pelvic fins under the belly.

HABITS

Pike are fierce predators and, not surprisingly, are usually found on their own. They often hide among weeds where they are well camouflaged. They wait for smaller fish to pass by. Perch live in shoals when they are small, but are often solitary when they grow large. Sticklebacks usually hide among water plants for protection.

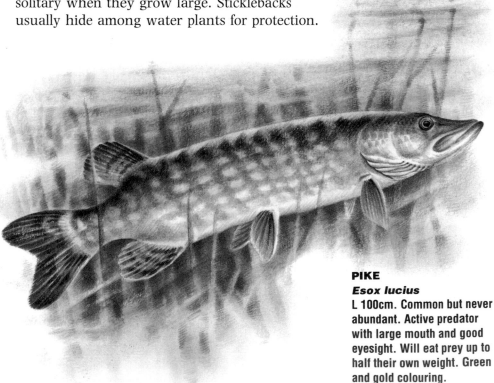

PIKE
Esox lucius
L 100cm. Common but never abundant. Active predator with large mouth and good eyesight. Will eat prey up to half their own weight. Green and gold colouring.

PERCH
Perca fluviatilis
L 30cm. Common and widespread. Dark stripes on body give good camouflage among weeds. Ventral fins are red.

**THREE-SPINED ▷
STICKLEBACK**
Gasterosteus aculeatus
L 5cm. Common and widespread. Females are silvery brown. In breeding season, males develop red belly and blue eyes.

**NINE-SPINED
STICKLEBACK**
Pungitius pungitius
L 4cm. Common and widespread. Breeding male has dark throat. Spawns in nest made by the male among weeds.

HOW TO WATCH

In the breeding season, male three-spined sticklebacks become bright red and blue. They guard a territory and build a nest of mud and weeds on the bottom of the pond. They drive off rival male sticklebacks and soon attract a female to the nest. Spawning takes place in the nest. The male looks after the eggs and keeps predators away. When the young hatch, he guards them until they are large enough to fend for themselves. You can watch this behaviour in a tank. Be sure to keep only one male in the tank. However, you can keep several females.

FROGS AND TOADS

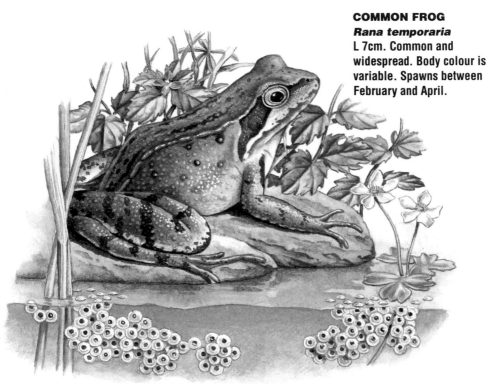

COMMON FROG
Rana temporaria
L 7cm. Common and widespread. Body colour is variable. Spawns between February and April.

HABITATS

Although frogs and toads can live on land, they have to return to water to breed. Common frogs can be found in many freshwater habitats: they often occur in garden ponds but are just as happy in lakes, canals and upland pools. Toads usually prefer wooded ponds and lakes, and can sometimes be seen in boggy pools.

HABITS

Frogs and toads are amphibians, which means they are equally at home on land and water. Toads, however, generally spend more time away from water than most frogs. Their skin is leathery and warty and they do not lose water so easily on dry land. On land a frog hops to escape danger, whereas a toad will walk.

Frogs mate and produce spawn in early spring. They usually return to the pond in which they were born, where large numbers often congregate and produce masses of frogspawn.

EDIBLE FROG
Rana esculenta
L 8cm. Beautifully marked frog. Males make loud croak. Introduced to southern England, but widespread on mainland Europe.

MARSH FROG ▲
Rana ridibunda
L 12cm. Body colour is usually greyish-brown with light green on back and small black patches. Largest frog in Europe.

PROJECT

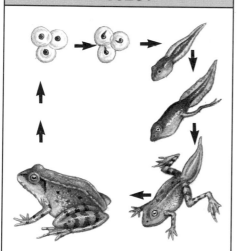

Collect a small amount of frogspawn, and put it in a large tank of water with pondweeds, away from direct sunlight. After hatching, the tadpoles grow their back legs first, followed by their front legs. The tail is gradually absorbed and the tadpole beings to look like a small frog. Note the time it takes to reach the different stages, and compare with the longer process in the wild.

▲ **COMMON TREE FROG**
Hyla arborea
L 4cm. Absent from Britain but widespread throughout mainland Europe. Often seen climbing plants.

▲ **COMMON TOAD**
Bufo bufo
L 8cm. Common and widespread. Warty skin. Often found away from water.

NEWTS AND SNAKES

PALMATE NEWT
Triturus helveticus
L 7cm. Breeding male has
webbed hind feet and thin
tail filament. Female similar
to smooth newt but with
unspotted throat.

CHARACTERISTICS

Like frogs and toads, newts are also amphibians.
As adults they can live just as well in water as
on land. However, they must return to the
water to breed. Newt tadpoles have feathery gills
and grow slowly. Grass snakes are reptiles. They
are often found in water but have to return to
the surface to breathe air. They lay their eggs
on land.

HABITS AND HABITATS

During the spring and summer months, newts
are found in ponds and lakes. They feed on pond
animals that live at the bottom and sometimes
hide among water plants. Newts swim well
when disturbed. In the autumn, most newts
leave their ponds and hibernate under logs and
bark. Grass snakes feed on frogs and fish. They
can swim well if alarmed.

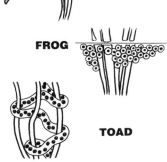

NEWT

FROG

TOAD

Newts lay their eggs on the
leaves of water plants. To
protect them, they use their
hind legs to wrap the leaf
around the egg. You can
sometimes watch them
doing this if you sit quietly
beside a pond in the spring.
Compare to frog and toad
spawn above.

SMOOTH NEWT
Triturus vulgaris
L 8cm. Common, widespread. Male has small crest on back. Female has spotted throat. Spends much time on land.

GREAT CRESTED NEWT ▶
Triturus cristatus
L 12cm. Very local. Usually in chalky ponds. Male has distinct crest along back. May remain in water throughout the year.

GRASS SNAKE
Natrix natrix
L 60cm. Widespread but not common today. Greenish colour with yellow 'collar'. Eggs are often laid in compost heaps.

HOW TO WATCH

Newt courtship is fascinating to watch. The behaviour can sometimes be seen in ponds and lakes. If you put palmate or smooth newts in a large tank they may also start to court, but always remember to return the newts to the pond where they came from. The male peforms an elaborate dance beside the female. The tail is curved round beside the body and vigorously waved. This carries his scent to the female. Do not try this observation with great crested newts. They are rare and protected by law and must not be removed from their ponds.

BIRDS

MUTE SWAN
Cygnus olor
L 150cm. Common and
unmistakable. Bill orange
with black knob at base.
Juveniles (cygnets) are fawn
coloured without a knob on
the beak.

HABITATS

Freshwater habitats are wonderful for birds and
birdwatchers. Swans, ducks, moorhens and
coots are often seen on open water on lakes,
gravel pits and canals. They usually nest in
vegetation around the margin of the lake or
pond. This gives them protection from land
predators. Tufted ducks and coots are sometimes
seen on reservoirs.

HABITS

Birds are found on fresh water because there is
good feeding. Mute swans use their long necks
to reach plants below the water surface.
Mallards and moorhens feed in shallow water.
Coots and tufted ducks dive to reach their food.
Coots make shallow dives and only stay
underwater for a short while. Tufted ducks may
stay under for 20 seconds or more.

The pintail is well named.
The male has long tail
feathers. It feeds by up-
ending in the water so that it
can reach food on the bottom
of the lake or pond.

MALLARD
Anas platyrhynchos
L 60cm. Common in all freshwater habitats. Female brown. Male has green head, chestnut breast and fawn body. Loud quacking call.

TUFTED DUCK ▼
Aythya fuligula
L 40cm. Common on reservoirs and lakes. Male is black and white with tufted head. Female is brown. Dives constantly.

MOORHEN ▲
Gallinula chloropus
L 30cm. Very common. Sometimes tame on urban lakes. Loud croaking call. Flicks tail showing white feathers.

PROJECT

If you sit beside a lake or gravel pit in the spring, you should see moorhens. If you wait long enough, you may see rival males fight. They grip each other by the feet and try to push their opponent underwater. Sometimes three or more do battle. See if you can count the number of birds and make a note of how often this happens.

COOT ▲
Fulica atra
L 40cm. Common and widespread. Black plumage and white bill and forehead characteristic. Lobed feet seen on land. Loud, screeching call.

BIRDS

KINGFISHER
Alcedo atthis
L 16cm. Unmistakable with bright blue and orange plumage. Widespread but not common. Nests in river bank holes.

HABITS

Grebes spend most of their lives on water. They are so well adapted to life on water that they have difficulty walking on land. Both species dive for fish. Kingfishers also catch fish but they plunge dive. Herons stalk their prey quietly in shallow water. Reed warblers and grey wagtails feed mainly on insects. Reed warblers are summer visitors.

HABITATS

Great crested grebes prefer open water such as lakes and gravel pits. Little grebes prefer streams and canals. Grey wagtails and kingfishers are also found in these habitats. Grey herons nest in trees but feed where there is shallow water or marshy ground. They feed on frogs and fish. Reed warblers build nests in reed-beds.

Great crested grebes build floating nests made of water plants and twigs. When the bird leaves the nest, it covers the eggs with nesting material to keep them concealed.

GREAT CRESTED GREBE
Podiceps cristatus
L 50cm. Common on large lakes. Performs courtship display in spring. Orange and black tufts present on face in spring. Dives for fish.

REED WARBLER ▼
Acrocephalus scirpaceus
L 12cm. Common in reed-beds in summer months. Loud scratchy song, sometimes sung from exposed spot. Cup-shaped nest woven in reed stems.

LITTLE GREBE ▲
Tachybaptus ruficollis
L 25cm. Common on clear streams and canals. May leave in winter. Trilling call. Chestnut cheeks in summer.

GREY WAGTAIL ▼
Motacilla cinerea
L 17cm. Common beside streams, rivers and watercress beds. Grey back and yellow underparts. Male has black throat.

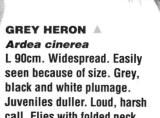

GREY HERON ▲
Ardea cinerea
L 90cm. Widespread. Easily seen because of size. Grey, black and white plumage. Juveniles duller. Loud, harsh call. Flies with folded neck.

AQUATIC MAMMALS

OTTER

Lutra lutra

L 110cm. Local and rare nowadays. The largest native mammal likely to be seen in British waters. Swims and dives well.

GENERAL FEATURES

Mammals are warm-blooded animals. To avoid losing too much heat, mammals that live in water often have thick fur. Sometimes there are two layers of fur. Only the outer layer gets wet. Otters are extremely good swimmers. They have webbed feet and can stay underwater for a long time. Water voles and water shrews can only dive for short periods.

HABITS

Otters and mink are fierce predators. They feed mainly on fish but will also take small mammals, ducklings and other birds if the opportunity arises. Water voles are vegetarians and eat the shoots of water plants. They build burrows in the side of the river bank. Water shrews are very active. They eat water insects and crustaceans.

When a water shrew dives, a layer of air is trapped in its fur. This makes it look like a silver bubble as it swims among the water plants. You can sometimes see this when you look down from a bridge to a stream where water shrews live.

WATER SHREW
Neomys fodiens
L 13cm. Locally common in streams, ditches and watercress beds. Distinguished by black upperparts and white underparts.

◁ WATER VOLE ▷
Arvicola terrestris
L 20cm. Becoming scarce. Usually seen sitting on river bank near entrance to burrows or swimming at surface. Dives when disturbed.

◁ AMERICAN MINK
Mustela vison
L 50cm. Originally escaped from fur farms but now established in the wild. Fierce predator. European mink now rare, found only in continental Europe.

MUSKRAT ▷
Ondatra zibethicus
L 60cm. Introduced from North America. Now found on continental Europe. Tail flattened from side to side. Feeds on water plants and small animals.

PLANTS

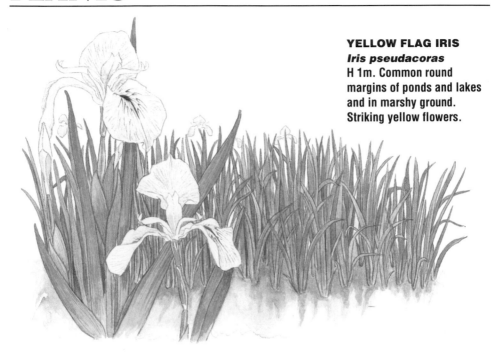

YELLOW FLAG IRIS
Iris pseudacoras
H 1m. Common round margins of ponds and lakes and in marshy ground. Striking yellow flowers.

GENERAL FEATURES

There are lots of freshwater plants in Britain and Europe. A typical plant has roots, a stem and green leaves. The roots anchor the plant in the ground, the stem supports the leaves, and the leaves themselves capture sunlight energy and make food. In order to reproduce, plants produce flowers and then seeds.

HABITATS

Most freshwater habitats are rich in plant life. Some species, such as water lilies, grow in the water. Others live at the edge of ponds, lakes and rivers and are called emergent plants. Most species of freshwater plants are completely adapted to the damp conditions. They cannot survive in dry soils elsewhere.

The flowers of yellow flag iris plants are pollinated by insects. The seeds are formed in three long capsules. As they ripen, they split to reveal the seeds.

OSIER WILLOW
Salix viminosa
H 10m. Grows in wet ditches and beside lakes and ponds. Leaves long, narrow and drooping. Catkins appear before leaves.

ALDER
Alnus glutinosa
H 15m. Common beside ponds and in damp woods. Leaves rounded. Catkins appear before leaves. Cone-like when mature.

WHITE WATER LILY
Nymphaea alba
L 20cm. Common in lakes and ponds. Flowers and circular leaves float. Roots anchored in bottom sediments.

SOFT RUSH
Juncus effusus
H 60cm. Common on damp ground and marshes. Round, leaf-like stems grow in clumps. Flowers produced in compact clusters.

REEDMACE
Typha latifolia
H 2m. Grows at margins of lakes, ponds and slow-flowing rivers. Flowers produced in brown, sausage-like clusters. Sometimes called bulrush.

PLANTS

GENERAL FEATURES

Some water plants, such as Canadian pondweed and hornwort, live completely submerged in water. Others have part of the plant in water and part above. Water mint and water milfoil have flowers produced on aerial spikes. The flowers of water starwort and hornwort are tiny and usually found underwater.

HABITATS

The plants on this page are found mainly in ponds, lakes and sometimes on backwaters beside slow-flowing rivers. Water starwort is a very variable plant which occurs in many other habitats. Some forms are even found in wet woodland hollows. In the winter, most of these plants die back. By the middle of the summer, they form dense growths.

All plants use sunlight energy to make food and they also produce oxygen. The process is called photosynthesis. If you put a piece of pondweed in a jar in bright sunlight, small bubbles of oxygen will soon appear on the leaves.

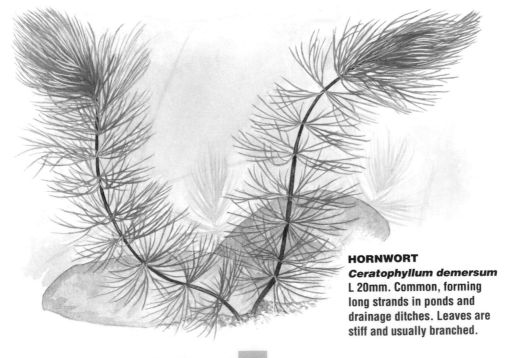

HORNWORT
Ceratophyllum demersum
L 20mm. Common, forming long strands in ponds and drainage ditches. Leaves are stiff and usually branched.

WATER MINT
Mentha aquatica
H 20cm. Common around ponds and in marshes. Leaves smell strongly of mint. Flowers produced in dense clusters.

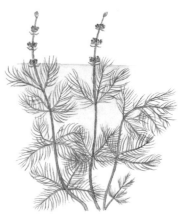

WATER STARWORT
Callitriche stagnalis
L 50cm. Common in a variety of habltats. Floating leaves form a star-shaped rosette. Grows in dense masses.

WATER MILFOIL
Myriophyllum spicatum
L 30cm. Common in lakes and slow-flowing rivers. Spikes of flowers early summer. Leaves arranged in whorls. Feathery appearance.

PROJECT

Fill three identical jars with (1) water from a chalk stream, (2) distilled water and (3) heathland water. Put ten leaves of duckweed in each. Duckweed divides as it grows. Count the number of leaves every week to compare which water suits the plant best. The water which contains the most nutrients will have the most duckweed.

CANADIAN PONDWEED
Elodea canadensis
L 50cm. Introduced species from North America. Now common in many lakes and ponds. Tough, curled leaves arranged in whorls of three to four.

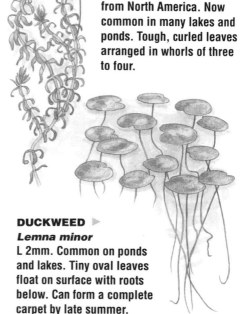

DUCKWEED
Lemna minor
L 2mm. Common on ponds and lakes. Tiny oval leaves float on surface with roots below. Can form a complete carpet by late summer.

PLANTS

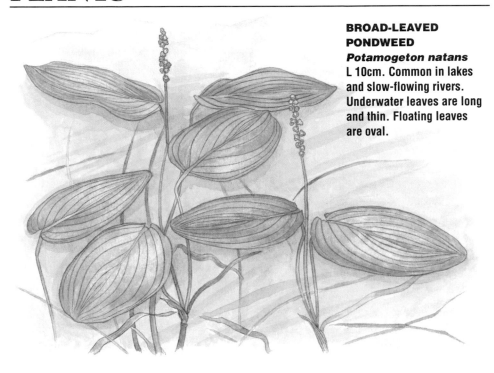

BROAD-LEAVED PONDWEED
Potamogeton natans
L 10cm. Common in lakes and slow-flowing rivers. Underwater leaves are long and thin. Floating leaves are oval.

GENERAL FEATURES

Unlike the other plants on this page, water horsetail is not a flowering plant. It produces spores instead of seeds. Broad-leaved pondweed and water crowfoot have leaves that grow underwater as well as at the surface. Depending on where they grow, the leaves look different even though they are on the same plant.

HABITAT

The common reed is a widespread and conspicuous water plant. It grows beside ponds, lakes, canals and rivers, and often covers large areas which are called reed-beds. Reed sweet-grass grows in similar habitats. There are several similar species of water crowfoot. The common one is found in ponds with broad-leaved pondweed and branched bur-reed.

In some areas, common reeds are cut and used to make thatched roofs on houses. This is a skilled craft. The thatch provides good heat insulation for the house.

WATER CROWFOOT
Ranunculus aquatilis
L 15mm. Common in ponds and ditches. Underwater leaves finely divided. Surface leaves are broad. Flowers have five petals.

BRANCHED BUR-REED
Sparganium erectum
H 60cm. Common in margins of ponds and marshes. Flowers have spherical heads. Male and female are separate.

COMMON REED
Phragmites australis
H 1.5m. Common in many freshwater habitats. Flowers and seeds in loose, grass-like heads. Plant green at first, turning brown.

REED SWEET-GRASS
Glyceria maxima
H 1m. Common around lakes and in ditches. Leaves are bright green. Flowers and seeds have loose heads.

WATER HORSETAIL
Equisetum fluviatile
H 1m. Locally common in shallow water. Regularly spaced nodes up bright green stem. Sometimes branched in places.

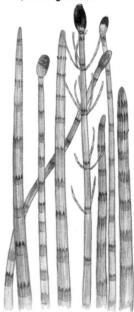

INDEX

ILLUSTRATIONS BY

Jim Channel 21, 26–27, 28–29, 30–31, 32–33, 34–35, 36–37, 38–39, 42–43 · Roger Kent
110–111 · Stephen Lings, 14–15, 114–115, 116–117 · Mick Loates 102–103, 104–105,
106–107, 108–109 · Alan Male 8–9, 54–77, 88–91 · Maltings Partnership 5, 10, 11, 12, 13,
16, 17, 19, 22, 23 · Jane Pickering 20, 120–125 · Phil Weare 4, 6–7, 24–25, 40–41, 44–53,
78–87, 92–101, 112–113, 118–119.
Additional black and white line illustrations by Jane Pickering.

**The publishers would like to thank the following organizations and
individuals for their kind permission to reproduce the photographs in
this book.**

Heather Angel 86, 109 · Nature Photographers Ltd: front cover; S C Bisserot 92,
Nicholas Brown 5, 74, 96, 100; Robin Bush 58; Colin Carver 35; Andrew Cleave 107;
Jean Hall 122; K Handford 18; Dr M R Hill 23, E A Janes 124; Paul Sterry 11, 17, 21,
25, 27, 31, 41, 44, 45, 46, 48, 50, 54, 56, 60, 61, 62, 63, 66, 67, 68, 76, 78, 79, 81, 90, 94, 98, 101,
102, 110, 113, 114, 115, 116, 123; Neil Wilmore 52 · NHPA: 106; G I Bernard 88, 99;
Stephen Dalton 37, 64, 71, 118; E A James 13; Michael Tweedie 87; David Woodfall
23.